# Campaigns and Conflicts

*Comparing Times and Cultures*

Play selection and
resource material by

### Steve Lewis

Series Consultant
Cecily O'Neill

**Dedicated to the memory of my dear friend Trisha Trail**

Published by Collins Educational, an imprint of HarperCollins*Publishers* Ltd, 77–85 Fulham Palace Road, London W6 8JB

> www.**Collins**Education.com
> On-line support for schools and colleges

© Selection and Activities copyright Steve Lewis 2003

First published 2003

ISBN 000 713143 7

Steve Lewis asserts the moral right to be identified as the author of this work.

All rights reserved. No part of this publication may be reproduced, stored in a retrieval system, or transmitted in any form or by any means, electronic, mechanical, photocopying, recording or otherwise, without either the prior permission of the Publisher or a licence permitting restricted copying in the United Kingdom issued by the Copyright Licensing Agency Ltd, 90 Tottenham Court Road, London W1P 9HE.

British Library Cataloguing in Publication Data

A catalogue record for this book is available from the British Library.

Commissioned by Isabelle Zahar, edited by Mitzi Bales and Mark Dudgeon, picture research by Mark Dudgeon and Gavin Jones.

Design and typesetting by Jordan Publishing Design, cover design by Jordan Publishing Design, cover photograph of *The Crucible* courtesy of 20th Century Fox.

**Acknowledgements**

The following permissions to reproduce material are gratefully acknowledged:

*Text:* Extract from *Lysistrata and Other Plays* translated by Alan H. Sommerstein, published by Penguin Classics, 1973 © Alan H. Sommerstein, 1973; from *Lysistrata*, translated by Dudley Fitts, published by Faber and Faber Ltd 1960; *Lysistrata* translated by Ranjit Bolt, reproduced by permission of The Agency (London) Ltd © 1999 by Ranjit Bolt; Excerpted from Patric Dickinson's translation of *Lysistrata* by Aristophanes © copyright 1957, 1996 the Estate of Patric Dickinson, reprinted by permission of the publishers: www.nickhernbooks.co.uk. All rights reserved; extract from *The Crucible* © Arthur Miller, c/o International Creative Management (New York); extract from *Oh What A Lovely War* © Joan Littlewood, published by Methuen; *Blighters* © Siegfried Sassoon, published by Faber and Faber Ltd; *Bombardment* by Richard Aldington, © The Estate of Richard Aldington; extract from *Stronger Than Superman* © Roy Kift; *The Bone Collector* by Jeffery Deaver, © Jeffery Deaver 1997, published by Hodder Uk; 'Lament for the Witches' from *Vinegar Tom* © Caryl Churchill.

*Images:* A Greek theatre © Richard Leacroft, p16; © Wendy Gough of Arlecchina's Masks, p17;

Every effort has been made to trace copyright holders, but in some cases this has proved impossible. The publishers would be happy to hear from any copyright holder that has not been acknowledged.

Production by Katie Morris, Printed and bound in Thailand by Imago.

> You might also like to visit
> www.**fire**and**water**.co.uk
> The book lover's website

# *Contents*

| | |
|---|---:|
| **Introduction** | 2 |
| GCSE Drama Coursework Coverage Charts | 3 |
| English Framework Objectives Chart | 5 |
| **Extract 1:** *Lysistrata* by Aristophanes | 6 |
| Staging the Extract | 16 |
| Exploring the Extract | 20 |
| Exploring Characters | 25 |
| Comparing Texts | 26 |
| **Extract 2:** *The Crucible* by Arthur Miller | 28 |
| Staging the Extract | 39 |
| Exploring the Extract | 42 |
| Exploring Characters | 45 |
| Comparing Texts | 47 |
| **Extract 3:** *Oh What a Lovely War* by Theatre Workshop and Charles Chilton | 49 |
| Staging the Extract | 64 |
| Exploring the Extract | 69 |
| Exploring Characters | 72 |
| Comparing Texts | 74 |
| **Extract 4:** *Stronger than Superman* by Roy Kift | 76 |
| Staging the Extract | 91 |
| Exploring the Extract | 94 |
| Exploring Characters | 97 |
| Comparing Texts | 104 |
| **Exploring and Comparing the Four Extracts** | 106 |

---

### KEY

71–74 / 71–74    cross-reference between playscript and teaching resources.

**H**    in resources = activity suitable for homework.

# Introduction

This is a collection of play extracts that show four very different approaches to the general theme of *Campaigns and Conflicts*.

- *Lysistrata* is an ancient Greek comedy where the women of Athens campaign for peace by refusing to have sex with their husbands until they stop the conflict with Sparta.
- *The Crucible* involves both a personal and political campaign in the form of a witch-hunt. Personal jealousies and old scores are settled in the 17th-century town of Salem in America when superstition about witches overcomes common sense.
- *Oh What a Lovely War* is a documentary in song and dance of the events of World War I. It demonstrates both the horror and stupidity of the war, but the voice of those campaigning for peace can barely be heard above the patriotic cries for victory at all costs.
- *Stronger than Superman* is a play that gives a voice to people who have to use a wheelchair to get around. It contends that "wheel-people" are just the same as those who get around with the use of their own legs. This play has been part of the international campaign to give disabled people the same rights as the able-bodied.

This selection of plays and resources are suitable for study, exploration and/or performance within the GCSE Drama specifications offered by AQA, Edexcel, OCR and WJEC. The extracts make complete short plays in their own right and can be used effectively for the performance component for any GCSE Drama course.

Each extract lasts between fifteen and twenty minutes.

Extract 1 (from *Lysistrata*) requires a cast of 5 females (3 named and a minimum of 2 in the female chorus) and 4 males (1 named and a minimum of 3 in the male chorus). (The Chorus can be made larger and all-male or all-female casts can perform the play.)

Extract 2 (from *The Crucible*) requires a cast of 2 females and 1 male.

Extract 3 (from *Oh What a Lovely War*) requires a minimum cast of 8 playing a number of different roles.

Extract 4 (from *Stronger than Superman*) requires a cast of 1 female and 3 males, but the gender of the characters can be altered if required.

# AQA DRAMA COURSEWORK COVERAGE CHART

Candidates taking the AQA GCSE Drama course must offer two different options for coursework: one from the list of Scripted Work options and one from the list of Unscripted Work options. At least one of these must be a performance option. Where a technical and design skill option is undertaken, it must contribute to a group performance. Each option is divided into three parts, with each part testing a different Assessment Objective (AO).

**AO1 Final presentation (either performance or demonstration/artefacts)**, in which candidates are assessed on their ability to *"demonstrate ability in and knowledge and understanding of the practical skills in drama necessary for the realisation of a presentation to an audience, working constructively with others."*

**AO2 Response to plays and other types of drama**, in which candidates are assessed on their ability to *"respond with knowledge and understanding to plays and other types of drama from a performance perspective and to explore relationships and comparisons between texts and dramatic styles of different periods and of different cultures in order to show an awareness of their social context and genre."*

**AO3 Work in progress**, in which candidates are assessed on their ability to *"analyse and evaluate the effectiveness of their own and others' work with sensitivity as they develop and present their work in an appropriate format for communication."*

| QA Coursework option | 1. *Lysistrata* | 2. *The Crucible* | 3. *Oh What a Lovely War* | 4. *Stronger than Superman* | Comparing the Four Extracts |
|---|---|---|---|---|---|
| Option 1: Devised thematic work | 1e; 1f; 1g | 2f | 3h; 3i; 3j; 3m | 4h; 4i | 5a; 5d; 5f |
| Option 2: Acting | 1g; 1i | 2f | 3h; 3l | 4h | 5a; 5b |
| Option 3: Improvisation | | 2g; 2h; 2j | | 4f; 4g; 4i | 5a; 5f |
| Option 5: Dance | | | p68 | 3 | |
| Option 6: Set | 1a | 2a | p64 | 4a | |
| Option 7: Costume | p18 | p40 | p64; 3a | 4b | |
| Option 8: Makeup | * | * | * | * | |
| Option 9: Properties | | 2b | | p92 | |
| Option 10: Masks | p17; 1b; 1h | | | | |
| Option 11: Puppets | N/A | N/A | N/A | N/A | |
| Option 12: Lighting | p19 | p41 | p65; 3b | p93 | |
| Option 13: Sound | | p41 | 3c; p67 | p93 | |
| Option 14: Stage Management | • | • | • | • | |

*Make-up can be used in all of these plays     • All these plays can be used as stage management texts

# EDEXCEL DRAMA COURSEWORK COVERAGE CHART

The chart below highlights which activities provide opportunities or guidance for work on the Edexcel Paper 1, Units 1 and 2: Drama Exploration. In the workshops for this paper, to be based around at least two different types of drama texts, candidates are required to use (a) at least four of the explorative strategies, (b) at least two of the drama skill areas and (c) to select and use appropriately the elements of drama in their practical and written responses to the stimulus material.

| Edexcel c/w strategies, skills and elements of drama | 1. Lysistrata | 2. The Crucible | 3. Oh What a Lovely War | 4. Stronger than Superman | Comparing the four extracts |
|---|---|---|---|---|---|
| (a) Explorative Strategies ||||||
| Still image | 1f | | 3m | 4e | |
| Thought-tracking | | 2f | 3i | 4e | |
| Narrating | 1g | | | | |
| Hot-seating | | 2h | | 4f | 5a |
| Role-play | | 2g | | 4g | |
| Cross-cutting | | | | 4h | |
| Forum theatre | 1e | | | | |
| Marking the moment | | | | | |
| (b) The Drama Medium ||||||
| Use of costume, masks, make-up | p17; 1b; p18; 1h | p40 | p64; 3a | p92; 4b | |
| Sound/music | | p41 | p66; 3c; p67 | p93 | |
| Lighting | p19 | p41 | p65; 3b | p93 | |
| Space/levels | | | | | |
| Set and props | p16; 1a | p39; 2a; 2b | p64 | p91; 4a; p92 | |
| Movement, mime, gesture | 1g | | p68 | | |
| Voice | 1c; 1g; 1h; 1i | 2f | 3h; 3j | 4j | |
| Spoken language | | | 3m | | |
| (c) The Elements of Drama ||||||
| Action/plot/content | 1f | 2d | | 4h | 5d; 5d |
| Forms | 1b; 1g; 1i | 2j | 3g | 4j | 5d; 5f |
| Climax/anticlimax | | 2d | | 4h | 5a; 5b; 5d |
| Rhythm/pace/tempo | | 2d | | 4h | 5a; 5b; 5d |
| Contrasts | | | 3k | | 5d; 5f |
| Characterisation | 1c; 1h | 2f; 2g; 2h | 3i; 3j | 4e; 4f; 4g; 4i | 5d |
| Conventions | 1b; 1g; 1i | | 3a; 3g; 3k | 4h; 4j | 5b; 5d |
| Symbols | | 2b | 3a; 3k | | 5d |

# Introduction

# ENGLISH FRAMEWORK OBJECTIVES CHART

| English Framework Objective | 1. Lysistrata | 2. The Crucible | 3. Oh, What a Lovely War | 4. Stronger Than Superman | Comparing the four extracts |
|---|---|---|---|---|---|
| Comment on the authorial perspectives offered in texts on individuals, community and society in texts from different cultures (R6) | 1d | 2c; 2i | 3h | 4c; 4k | 5a; 5c; 5f |
| Compare the presentation of ideas, values or emotions in related or contrasting texts (R7) | 1j | 2i | 3k | 4k | 5c |
| Analyse the language, form and dramatic impact of scenes and plays by published dramatists (R14) |  | 2e |  | 4h | 5b |
| Analyse ways in which different cultural contexts and traditions have influenced language and style (R16) | * | *<br>2e | *<br>3f | * | * |
| Make telling use of descriptive detail (W11) | 1g |  |  | 4j |  |
| Recognise, evaluate and extend the skills and techniques they have developed through drama (S&L11) | 1c |  | 3g; 3k | 4e; 4f; 4g |  |
| Use a range of drama techniques, including work in role, to explore issues, ideas and meanings (S&L12) | 1e; 1f; 1g | 2f, 2g; 2h | 3i; 3j | 4e; 4f; 4g; 4h; 4i | 5f |
| Develop and compare different interpretations of scenes or plays by Shakespeare or other dramatists (S&L13) |  | 2j |  |  |  |
| Convey action, character, atmosphere and tension when scripting and performing plays (S&L14) | 1h; 1k | 2d; 2d | 3l | 4j | 5d; 5f |

5

> **EXTRACT 1**

# Lysistrata
## Aristophanes

### ARISTOPHANES

Aristophanes was born about 445 BC and died in about 385 BC. He was writing comedies at the same time as the great playwrights, Sophocles and Euripides, were writing tragedies and his plays are the only known examples representing this oldest form of Greek Comedy. He was born to a wealthy man but worked prodigiously to produce 40 plays. Only 11 of these survive. His first known play, *Banqueters*, was produced in 427 BC when he was in his early 20s. This won second prize in a contest and established his reputation. Among the plays that have survived, the best known are *Clouds, Frogs, Wasps, Peace* and *Lysistrata*. *Lysistrata* was first performed in Athens at the Lenean Festival in 411 BC. His most creative period was at a time of civil war between Athens and Sparta (431 BC–404 BC) and this period of conflict provides the background for *Lysistrata* as well as many of his other plays.

### SUMMARY OF THE PLOT

The women of Greece have decided that the only way to stop the civil war between Athens and Sparta is to force the men of both city-states to stop fighting. Lysistrata has two ideas to bring the war to an end. Her first idea is to get all the Greek women to agree to withhold all sexual favours from their husbands. Her second idea is for the women of Athens to seize the Acropolis where all the money of the state is kept, so that the rulers would not be able to pay the army. At the start of the play, Lysistrata is waiting for the women to arrive so that she can tell them her plans. Eventually, the women agree to the sex strike and they swear an oath together on a phallic wineskin.

The next scene of the play involves the attempt by the old men of Athens to recapture the Acropolis but they soon retreat when the women pour water over them. A City Magistrate then attempts to get the women out of the Acropolis. Lysistrata comes out of the Acropolis to discuss matters with the Magistrate, who tries to assert male supremacy. The women humble him by dressing him up as a woman and carrying out a funeral ceremony as if he were dead.

After a section in which the Chorus of Old Men and the Chorus of Old Women confront each other, Lysistrata expresses concern that many of her followers are beginning to weaken and slip away to see their husbands. She manages to convince them to continue with their sex strike. The Chorus of Old Men and the Chorus of Old Women resume their insults until a young soldier, Kinesias (whose name means *randy*) arrives. In the following scene, Kinesias experiences growing sexual frustration as his wife, Myrrhine, teases him with the promise of sex only to withdraw it when he refuses to agree to peace. Finally, an ambassador from Sparta arrives to discuss peace with the Athenians. The men still are unable to agree until Lysistrata shows them how to make peace. The play ends in a celebration of song and dance.

## THE SCENE IN CONTEXT

This extract is the scene in which the Magistrate confronts Lysistrata and the women outside the Acropolis.

# *Lysistrata*

By
## Aristophanes – Ancient Greece
Translated by Patric Dickinson*

### CAST IN ORDER OF APPEARANCE

MAGISTRATE – an official of the City of Athens
LYSISTRATA – leader of the women's revolt
KALONIKE – friend to Lysistrata
MYRRHINA – friend to Lysistrata
CHORUS OF MEN – old men of Athens
CHORUS OF WOMEN – friends to Lysistrata

(The Chorus of Men requires a minimum of three performers who can also play the Officers. The Chorus of Women requires a minimum of two performers. Kalonike and Myrrhina can also be part of the Chorus of Women).

### Setting
*The scene takes place before the gates of the Acropolis in the City of Athens.*

## Scene One

MAGISTRATE   And now here am I, a government official,
Come to get money out of the Treasury
To pay for oars, and the gates are barricaded
Right in my face by these rampant women!
I must put a stop to this nonsense.
Fetch me crowbars! Why are you goggling

---

* Published in 1996 by Nick Hern Books, ISBN 1 85459 325 0

There, you slacker? Snooping about for an inn?
Crowbars! Shove these crowbars under the gates:
You, over *there*! I'll take this. Now. One – two – three –

*But the gates open and there stands* **Lysistrata**.

| | |
|---|---|
| **Lysistrata** | You needn't force the gates. I'm coming out<br>Of my own accord – and it isn't crowbars you want,<br>It's common sense. |
| **Magistrate** | Really? You … You – where's my officer?<br>Arrest her! Tie her hands behind her back. |
| **Lysistrata** | By Artemis! The tip of a finger on me,<br>And public servant or not, his private service<br>'ll be over! |
| **Magistrate** *(to his men)* | Are you afraid? You there, go with him,<br>Tackle her round the waist, tie her up, get on with it! |

*Enter* **Kalonike**

| | |
|---|---|
| **Kalonike** | By Hekate! A finger on *her* and I'll spread<br>Your guts on the road! |
| **Magistrate** | My guts on the road, eh?<br>Officer! Handcuff this one! She talks too much. |

*Enter* **Myrrhine**

| | |
|---|---|
| **Myrrhine** | By Phosphoros, the tip of a finger tip<br>On *her*, and it's two lovely black eyes … |
| **Magistrate** | What's all this? *Officer!* Arrest them!<br>I'm warning you, we can't *have* this sort of thing. |
| **Lysistrata** | I'm warning *you*:<br>We're four companies fully armed and ready. |

**CAMPAIGNS AND CONFLICTS**

**MAGISTRATE**  Not an officer left. But I'll be damned
If I'll be downed by women! Scythians!
Close ranks and prepare to charge!

**LYSISTRATA**  Come on, everyone!
Sling 'em, fling 'em, bang 'em, slang 'em!
Do your worst! *(The women attack the men.)*
Enough! Back there!
Enough! Don't strip the dead.

**MAGISTRATE** *(gloomily)*  A gory time for my men, and no mistake.

**LYSISTRATA**  Did you think it was *slaves* you came to fight?
Don't you imagine women thirst for glory?

**MAGISTRATE**  You *thirst* all right, if there's a bar in sight.

*The two **Choruses** face each other again.*

**CHORUS OF MEN** *(to **Magistrate**)*
Hey, you old windbag!
Call yourself one of our rulers?
What's the point of negotiating
With wild beasts?
Don't you know
What sort of a wetting they gave us?

**CHORUS OF WOMEN**  Was it right to attack
Your neighbours without a reason?
If you do, you must take
Whatever you get – black eyes!
All *I* want to do
Is to sit like a good little virgin,
Meek and mild at home,
Not moving a muscle, *but if you*
*Stir up a wasps' nest, be prepared for stings!*

**CHORUS OF MEN**  O Zeus, what shall we do with these dragons?
I can't put up with this! Let's probe
Into this shocking affair:
*Why* did they want to seize
This Kranaan, inaccessible,
Holy Acropolis up on the rock?

*(to **Magistrate**)*

> Question them, then; take nothing for granted;
> Cross-examine them closely;
> It'd be culpable negligence not
> To get to the bottom of this!

**MAGISTRATE**   Then first I want to ask: why lock us out of the citadel?

**LYSISTRATA**   To keep the money safe – so you don't go on fighting for it.

**MAGISTRATE**   Is money the cause of the war?

**LYSISTRATA**   Yes, and of every disturbance.
Peisander – anyone – who's ever got into power:
They always stir up trouble, then they can get at the money,
And do what they like with it. Now, not a penny more!

**MAGISTRATE**   What are you going to do?

**LYSISTRATA**   Control the Exchequer.

**MAGISTRATE**   Control the Exchequer, *you*!

**LYSISTRATA**   Is that so funny?
*We* do the housekeeping.

**MAGISTRATE**   That isn't the same.

**LYSISTRATA**   Why isn't it?

**MAGISTRATE**   This money's for *war* purposes –

**LYSISTRATA**   But that's precisely our point: No – more – war.

**MAGISTRATE**   Then how shall we save the city?

**LYSISTRATA**   We'll save you!

**MAGISTRATE**   You?

**LYSISTRATA**   That's what I said.

**Magistrate** Monstrous!

**Lysistrata** Whether you like it or not.

23 **Magistrate** Ridiculous nonsense!

**Lysistrata** *Why* get so cross? That *is* what's going to happen.

**Magistrate** Preposterous!

**Lysistrata** We *must* save you.

**Magistrate** Suppose I don't want to be?

**Lysistrata** All the more reason to.

**Magistrate** What's made you dabble
In these matters of peace and war?

**Lysistrata** If you listen, I'll tell you.

**Magistrate** You'd better be brief – or you'll catch it.

**Lysistrata** Then do *listen* and try to stop clenching your fists.

**Magistrate** Dammit, I *can't*! You make me so irritable!

**Chorus of Women** *(mocking him)* You'd *better* try – or you'll catch it!

**Magistrate** Be quiet, you old crow! *(to **Lysistrata**)* You speak.

27 **Lysistrata** Thank you.
All through the war – and what a long war –
By controlling ourselves we managed to endure
Somehow what you men did. We never once
Let ourselves grumble. Not that we approved
What you did do – simply, we understood you.
Oh, how often at home one would hear you spouting
Hot air about something serious! And masking
Our misery with a smile we'd ask you gently,
"Dear, in the Assembly today, did you decide
*Anything* about peace?" And, "What's that to do with *you*,"
You'd growl. "Shut up!" And I did.

**MAGISTRATE**   You'd have been sorry if you hadn't
Well …

**LYSISTRATA**   I held my tongue. And immediately you'd make
Some even more crazy decision, and I'd sigh
 and say,
"But how *can* you have passed this lunatic
 thing?"
And you'd frown and mutter, "Stick to your
 spinning,
Or you *will* have something to complain of.
War is men's business."

**MAGISTRATE**   And quite right too!

**LYSISTRATA**   Shouldn't we try to save you from your follies?
When we see you mooning about in the streets
 moaning
"Isn't there a *man* left in this country?" "Not one,"
Says the old blimp with you. So we called a rally
Of all the women and planned: *we* would save
 Greece.
Why wait any longer? Now you must listen to
 *us* –
It's our turn to talk, and *yours* to be quiet as
 we've been,
While *we're* busy, putting things right again.

**MAGISTRATE**   You do that for *us*! Intolerab –

**LYSISTRATA**   SILENCE!

**MAGISTRATE**   Told to be quiet by a woman in a veil,
I'd rather die …

**LYSISTRATA**   Oh, if *that's* all it is –
*You* put my veil on *your* head and be QUIET!
 (*She puts it on him.*)

**KALONIKE**   And here's a spindle.
She forces it into his hand.

**MYRRHINE**   And a *dear* little wool-basket.

**LYSISTRATA**  Now bundle up your skirt, card wool, and chew beans –
　　　　　　　　War is women's work!

*The **Magistrate** is reduced to impotent silence.*

**CHORUS OF WOMEN**  Come on, women, put down our pitchers and take the field,
　　　　　　　　We must do our proper bit for the common cause!
　　　　　　　　Never shall I stop dancing,
　　　　　　　　Never my knees give,
　　　　　　　　Nothing I wouldn't dare
　　　　　　　　For comrades of such metal,
　　　　　　　　Such spirit and grace and flair,
　　　　　　　　Such wisdom and love of country,
　　　　　　　　And such entrancing *sense*!
　　　　　　　　Born of mettlesome mothers, sharp to molest as nettles,
　　　　　　　　Let us advance righteous, in anger, and never yield:
　　　　　　　　The wind stands fair!

**LYSISTRATA**  *(as in prayer)*
　　　　　　　　But let sweet-spirit Love, let Aphrodite breathe
　　　　　　　　On our breasts and thighs today
　　　　　　　　And enflame delight, and quicken
　　　　　　　　The men to desire, that we
　　　　　　　　May be called by all the Greeks
　　　　　　　　Peacemakers.

# GLOSSARY

**Lysistrata** – pronounced liss-i-STRAH-ta and meaning "releaser of armies"

**Kalonike** – pronounced kal-on-EE-kee and meaning "fine victory"

**Myrrhine** – pronounced mi-REE-nee and meaning "myrtle wreath" or "sexpot"

**Artemis** – goddess of childbirth; of virginity; of the moon; of wild animals and protector of women

**Hekate** – goddess of black magic, often represented with three bodies or three heads

**Phosphoros** – the name given to Artemis as the goddess of the moon

**Scythians** –people from Scythia in the northern part of Greece. They were very good archers and made up a large part of the police force of Athens.

**Zeus** – the father of the gods and of humankind; the ruler of the universe

**Kranaan** – another name for the Acropolis

**Acropolis** – the fortress on a rocky hill in Athens

**citadel** – a fortress within a city that is a place of safety

**Peisander** – a scheming Greek politician who plotted the overthrow of democratic government in Athens at the time Aristophanes was writing

**exchequer** – the treasury department of the government

**blimp** – an officer in the military who is often portrayed as being stupid and reactionary

**Aphrodite** – goddess of beauty, love and sex

# Staging the extract

##  SET DESIGN

*Lysistrata* was originally performed in the large outdoor Theatre of Dionysos in Athens, which seated over 14,000 people. The audience was arranged in a fan-like shape around a central circular area known as the *orchestra* or place for dancing. The Chorus performed within this central arena, behind which was a long rectangular stage that may have had buildings or some kind of scenery placed on it. The principal characters performed mostly on this raised stage area. The extract takes place before the gates of the Acropolis through which Lysistrata makes her entrance, so very little scenery is required. All that is really needed is a pair of central gates that open out onto a central space in which the action of the scene can take place.

# Lysistrata

## ♦1a  Set Design activity   H

- Put together a collage of images of Ancient Greek buildings (built before the 5th-century BC). Look for images of buildings with gates, columns and different kinds of floors. Be aware of mosaic patterns, wall paintings and statues.

- Research the kind of rocks found in the Acropolis, noting shapes, colour and texture. Search the Internet and look in travel brochures to find modern day photographs of the Acropolis and the remains of the Parthenon.

- Create a scale model of a backdrop of a wall with gates using colours, textures, shapes and ideas selected from the range of research material you have collected. Extend this idea to create a covering for the floor in front of the backdrop.

- Consider setting the scene in a different period or country. How would you design the set in this case?

- The play takes place during a time of war. How might you suggest a war-torn city in the set? Collect photographs of towns and cities torn by bombs and battles to help you in developing visual ideas for the setting.

- How could you show through the setting that the women of Athens have taken over the Acropolis?

## MASKS

One of the particular features of Greek drama is that all of the actors wore masks. Originally these masks were made of wood with linen fabric stretched over them. The mouth section was built out at the front so that it would act as a loud hailer to carry the actor's voice around the theatre. Each mask was different in design so that the audience could immediately recognize each character. A particular feature of the masks was the extended forehead surrounded

*Comic mask for a woman*

with hair. The hair was coloured and shaped to suit the character it was meant to portray.

## ♦1b Mask activity

- Investigate different methods of making masks and decide which method you are going to use.
- Draw an outline of a face on a sheet of A4 paper, producing one for every character in the play. Write the name of each character at the top of each sheet (Lysistrata, Kalonike, Myrrhine, Magistrate, Police Officer, Chorus of Men, Chorus of Women). Discuss each character, writing down words that describe something about the character.
- If you intend to make a realistic mask, it is useful to collect a range of facial images that could give you ideas for representing various face types to link these to the "word-masks" you have created in the previous exercise. You could also include photographs of the actors who are going to be wearing the masks.
- Sketch ideas for each of the masks using the research material you have gathered. Try scanning different photographs of faces into a computer and using drawing software to change the shape of the head and facial features as well as adding hair. This is rather like a police photo-fit picture.
- Make each mask by the method you decided on earlier. It is important to ensure that the mask fits the actor's face, that it is comfortable and safe to wear, that it is secure and that the actor's voice can be clearly heard.

## COSTUMES

The costumes will need to be linked to the masks if they are used. With or without masks, the costumes can be as simple or as extravagant as your budget will allow. Decide if you are going to set the play at the time it was written in Ancient Greece or in a different period. This will require research into what women wore and the sort of uniform or badge of office that a magistrate might have worn. One of the important things is to show that the women in the play are exciting and the men are relatively dull. The use of colour could reflect this. Kalonike describes their clothes in an earlier scene as: "Sitting as pretty as flowers/ In our saffron silks, and all made up, and moulded/In the long folds of our gowns and our feet in dainty shoes." Lysistrata adds that she is counting on their "diaphanous nothings" as a weapon. What sort of clothing does this suggest to you? Above all, costumes in the play need to be bold and fun.

 **LIGHTING**

The play was originally performed in the open air in bright sunlight, so keep the scene as brightly lit as possible to suggest both the real heat of Athens and the heat generated by the passions and arguments of the characters.

# *Exploring the extract*

## HISTORICAL AND CULTURAL CONTEXT

There are two important things to realize about the historical and cultural context of the play:

1. The Peloponnesian War between Athens and Sparta had lasted 20 years when the play was written and went on for another seven years until Athens was eventually forced to surrender.

2. There were no women in Greek government at the time, no women actors and women were not allowed to attend plays. The play was originally performed by an all-male cast to an all-male audience.

## GENRE AND SUBJECT MATTER

*Lysistrata* is known as Aristophanic Comedy, a kind of comedy that uses a fantastical plot and makes fun of serious ideas and politicians. There are also elements of slapstick comedy in the play, for instance, where the women dress the Magistrate in women's clothes.

The subject matter of the play is deeply serious in that it deals with the frustration of a society that is engaged in a seemingly endless war. Everyone in the city-state of Athens has experienced the loss of a loved one in the pointless killing and fighting going on around them. Lysistrata decides that, as women are successful at managing their households, they could also manage to govern successfully. To the audience of the day, the idea of women running the affairs of state would have been completely ridiculous. But in the context of the play, Aristophanes is saying that it is no more ridiculous than the inability of men in power to end the war.

## ◆1c  The battle of the sexes

Look at the section of dialogue that begins:

MAGISTRATE:  What are you going to do?

And ends with the line:

MAGISTRATE:  Dammit, I can't! You make me so irritable.

This shows the contrast between the male and female attitudes in the play. The Magistrate is outraged and incensed while Lysistrata is calm and reasonable. Run the section through with the Magistrate shouting all of his lines and with Lysistrata saying her lines softly and quietly. What effect does this have on the audience and on the characters?

## ◆1d  Research and discussion

- Find out what you can about the long war between Sparta and Athens that raged from 431 BC to 404 BC.
- Find out what you can about the role of women in 5th-century BC Greek society.
- Discuss the following issues:
    - What would life have been like for Athenian women with their husbands, sons, fathers and brothers away at the war?
    - What sort of response was likely from the male audience of the day to the radical ideas in the play?
    - How might the role of women differ today if war were declared?

## ◆1e  Forum theatre

This exercise is aimed at exploring whether the situation in the extract could be resolved if the characters behaved differently.

*cont...*

**CAMPAIGNS AND CONFLICTS**

*Work as a whole group*

*Organization:* The group sits in a large circle. Three volunteers go into the centre of the circle as Group A and three volunteers go into the centre of the circle as Group B. Group A are workers in a factory and Group B are the managers/owners of the factory. You will need to decide what kind of factory it is.

*Situation:* Group A has had enough of poor wages, no career prospects and little or no appreciation of the work they do and have decided to go on strike. Group B arrives at the factory to find themselves locked out and Group A barricaded inside.

*Opening lines:* **MEMBER OF GROUP B:** Will one of you lot open this gate right now!
**MEMBER OF GROUP A:** Tell us why we should.

At any point in the improvisation, one of the performers can stop the action and ask the Forum for help or advice about what to do or say next. You can continue the improvisation from the point of interruption or start it again at any point you decide. Anyone from the Forum can also stop the improvisation if they think any character is doing or saying something inappropriate or unhelpful. However, if you as a Forum member stop the improvisation, you must **either** be prepared to go into the centre of the circle and take over one of the roles **or** make positive suggestions to the performers about what they might say or do differently. You also have to tell the performers where you want the improvisation to start from again. The improvisation continues until agreement is reached and the strike ends.

*Evaluation:* How does this situation parallel the circumstances in the extract? What does the exercise tell you about two groups of people in dispute with each other? How was the situation satisfactorily resolved?

◆1f **Still-images**

There are a number of important actions in the extract that communicate the hostility between the men and women. The purpose of this exercise is to demonstrate the actions through a series of still-images that tell the story visually.

# Lysistrata

*Organization:* Working as a group of at least six people, create the following still-images to illustrate each of the physical moments from the extract. One person in the group should cue the changes from one image to the next by saying the next number.

1. The Magistrate instructs an Officer to arrest Lysistrata but she threatens the Officer if he attempts to lay a hand on her.    9
2. The Magistrate instructs another Officer to tackle Lysistrata around the waist but this time Kalonike threatens to spill his guts on the road.    9
3. The Magistrate instructs yet another Officer to handcuff Kalonike, but this time Myrrhine threatens to give him two lovely black eyes.    9
4. The Magistrate and the Officers prepare to charge Lysistrata and the women.    10
5. The women attack the men.    10
   a. First blow    Create a series of freeze-frames showing the
   b. Second blow    women in different attack positions with the
   c. Third blow    men defending themselves.
6. The women defeat the men.    10
7. The men retreat.    10
8. The Magistrate questions Lysistrata.    11
9. The Magistrate loses his temper.    12
10. Lysistrata calmly tells the Magistrate that it is "our turn to talk and yours to be quiet."    13
11. The Magistrate loses his temper. Again.    13
12. The women dress the Magistrate up as a woman, giving him a veil, some knitting and a basket.    13

◆1g **Narrating**

Each of the headings in the still-image exercise provides an outline of the main events in the extract. Use these headings to create a narration for the scene. Add lines where and when you feel it is necessary.

*cont...*

**CAMPAIGNS AND CONFLICTS**

> *Organization:* One person takes on the role of the Narrator and the rest of the group divides into two. Group A represents Lysistrata and the women; Group B represents the Magistrate and the men.
>
> *Situation:* The Narrator slowly speaks the narration while Groups A and B act out in mime the event being described.
>
> *Extension:* Rehearse the narration and mime sequences so that they tell the story of the scene effectively.

# Exploring characters

Wearing masks calls for a non-naturalistic approach to the style of acting and to the representation of characters. The characters in the play are two-dimensional and deal more with ideas than with real emotions. They have broad and obvious personality traits rather than subtle characteristics with psychological depth.

◆1h **Mask work**

The following is the start of a list of words to describe each of the characters. Continue the list by adding descriptive words of your own.

| Lysistrata | Magistrate | Kalonike | Myrrhine |
|---|---|---|---|
| Independent | Officious | Aggressive | Sexy |
| Intelligent | Pompous | Agreeable | Alluring |
| Strong-minded | Affronted | Strong | Passionate |

Act out sections of dialogue in the manner that each descriptive word suggests. Act out the whole scene and find the most appropriate description or combination of descriptions that fit your role.

*Extension:* Repeat the exercise wearing masks. You will need to select a mask and stand in front of a mirror with it on. As you speak the lines, watch what happens to the mask in the mirror. You need to be able to see yourself in the mask at all times. You will need to spend some time wearing the mask and become aware of how it expresses what you are saying and the way you are saying it. Imagine that the mirror is your audience. Gradually you can move away from the mirror and start to work with the other masked actors.

CAMPAIGNS AND CONFLICTS

### ◆1i  Chorus work

**As a group**

Look at the section beginning:

**CHORUS OF MEN:**  Hey, you old windbag!

And concluding with the line:

**CHORUS OF MEN:**  To get to the bottom of this!

Consider the following questions:

**A.** How many actors are you going to have in each of the Male and Female Choruses?

**B.** How will the lines be spoken? Will you assign different lines to individual actors? Will you speak some or all of the lines in unison?

**C.** What sort of voice will you use? Will you speak in an accent?

**D.** How will each Chorus move? Will the groups stand tightly together or be spaced out? Where will the Male Chorus be placed in relation to the Female Chorus?

Experiment with different solutions to these questions.

## COMPARING TEXTS

This is the only play in this collection that has been translated from another language. There are many versions of the play in English but only one in the original Ancient Greek. When it comes to making the play work in English, translators have to make some adaptations. Here is a section of the extract in different versions.

| Translation 1<br>Alan H. Somerstein, 1973 | Translation 2<br>Dudley Fitts, 1960 | Translation 3<br>Ranjit Bolt, 1999 |
|---|---|---|
| **LYSISTRATA**  In the last war we were too modest to object to anything you men did – and in any case you wouldn't let us say a | **LYSISTRATA**  Ever since this war began we women have been watching you men, agreeing with you, keeping our thoughts to | **LYSISTRATA**  Very well – since history began War has been waged exclusively by man; Women looked on but took no part, because |

| word. But don't think we approved! We knew everything that was going on. | ourselves. That doesn't mean we were happy: we weren't, for we saw how things were going; but we'd listen to you at dinner arguing this way and that. | They recognized madness for what it was! You never let us state our point of view, But don't imagine we were fooled by you: We saw your antics, housebound though we were, And, though resigned to them, did not concur. |

◆1j **Discussion**

Find the corresponding speech by Lysistrata in the version used in the extract so that you have four versions to compare.

Consider the similarities and differences between these translations. Is the sense altered in any way?

How would you define the difference between translation and adaptation? Which version of this dialogue do you prefer and why?

◆1k **Writing**

The version by Ranjit Bolt is in rhyming couplets. Choose a section of the extract and write your own version of the scene using a rhyme scheme of your own.

Set the play in a particular region of the country and adapt the dialogue in that regional accent. You could try: Yorkshire, Somerset, Cornish, Welsh, Irish, Scottish, Liverpudlian, Geordie, Black Country, Bristolian or your own regional accent.

# The Crucible
## Arthur Miller

### ARTHUR MILLER

Arthur Miller was born on 17 October 1915 in New York City. Miller's father was a prosperous textile factory owner, but the wealth of the family declined when the business foundered during the Depression of 1929. Miller captures the experience of living through the Wall Street Crash and the subsequent Depression in his play, *The American Clock*, written much later in 1980. Miller began writing plays as a student at the University of Michigan from which he graduated in 1938. His first professionally produced play, *The Man Who Had All the Luck* (1944), was not a critical success and lasted less than a week on Broadway. It took Miller three years to return to playwriting and in Elia Kazan he found the perfect director for his next two prize-winning plays, *All My Sons* (1947) and *Death of A Salesman* (1949). *The Crucible* was written in 1953 and has since become Miller's most frequently produced play both in the United States and around the world.

### SUMMARY OF THE PLOT

*The Crucible* is based on historical events that took place in Salem, Massachusetts in 1692. Arthur Miller describes the central image he had of the play as "… that of a guilt-ridden man, John Proctor, who, having slept with his teenage servant girl, watches with horror as she becomes the leader of the witch-hunting pack and points her accusing finger at the wife he has himself betrayed."

This campaign by Abigail Williams to win John Proctor by accusing his wife, Elizabeth, of witchcraft is central to the play, but it is told against what was happening to others in the town of Salem.

The play opens with Betty Parris ill in bed, apparently in a trance but there seems to be no medical reason for her condition. Reverend Hale arrives and forces the Parris's black nurse, Tituba, to say that she has had dealings with the devil. The rumours of witchcraft spread like wildfire, creating hysteria and fear.

Abigail takes advantage of the witch-hunt to get rid of Elizabeth by denouncing her. In trying to save his wife, John is forced into confessing his adultery with Abigail. Elizabeth doesn't hear John's testimony and, when questioned about her husband's guilt, she lies to save his honour. John is condemned as being in league with the devil.

In the last act, John is faced with the stark choice between life based on a lie and death as an honest man. If he lies and confesses to being a wizard, he may live. If he remains true to himself and refuses to confess, he will be hanged. Proctor signs the confession but tears it up when he realizes that this lie will be posted in public on the church door. He goes to the gallows saying: "For now I do think I see a shred of goodness in John Proctor."

## THE SCENE IN CONTEXT

This extract is taken from Act Two of the play. John Proctor has just returned from work on his land. It is nearly dark and his wife, Elizabeth, has been singing their children to sleep. John has just eaten and is standing at the door looking up at the night sky. This extract is followed by the arrest of Elizabeth and ends with John physically threatening Mary Warren into going to the court with him in order to save Elizabeth from hanging.

# *The Crucible*

By
## Arthur Miller – USA

## CAST LIST

**JOHN PROCTOR** – a farmer in his middle thirties
**ELIZABETH PROCTOR** – wife to John
**MARY WARREN** – 18-year-old servant girl to the Proctor's.

### Setting
*The scene takes place in the common room of Proctor's house, Salem, Massachusetts, in the spring of the year 1692. At the right is a door opening on the fields outside. A fireplace is at the left, and behind it is a stairway leading upstairs. It is the low, dark, and rather long living-room of the time.*

## Scene One

*Elizabeth is watching Proctor from the table as he stands there absorbing the night. It is as though she would speak but cannot. Instead, now, she takes up his plate and glass and fork and goes with them to the basin. Her back is turned to him. He turns to her and watches her. A sense of their separation rises.*

**PROCTOR** I think you're sad again. Are you?

**ELIZABETH** *(she doesn't want friction, and yet she must)* You come so late I thought you'd gone to Salem this afternoon.

**PROCTOR** Why? I have no business in Salem.

**ELIZABETH** You did speak of going, earlier this week.

**Proctor** *(He knows what she means.)* I thought better of it since.

**Elizabeth** Mary Warren's there today.

**Proctor** Why'd you let her? You heard me forbid her to go to Salem anymore!

**Elizabeth** I couldn't stop her.

**Proctor** *(holding back a full condemnation of her)* It is a fault, it is a fault, Elizabeth – you're the mistress here, not Mary Warren.

**Elizabeth** She frightened all my strength away.

**Proctor** How may that mouse frighten you, Elizabeth? You –

**Elizabeth** It is a mouse no more. I forbid her go, and she raises up her chin like a daughter of a prince and says to me, "I must go to Salem, Goody Proctor; I am an official of the court!"

**Proctor** Court! What court?

**Elizabeth** Aye, it is a proper court they have now. They've sent four judges out of Boston, she says, weighty magistrates of the General Court, and at the head sits the Deputy Governor of the Province.

**Proctor** *(astonished)* Why, she's mad.

**Elizabeth** I would to God she were. There be fourteen people in the jail now, she says.

*Proctor simply looks at her, unable to grasp it.*

And they'll be tried, and the court have power to hang them too, she says.

**Proctor** *(scoffing, but without conviction)* Ah, they'd never hang –

**Elizabeth** The Deputy Governor promise hangin' if they'll not confess, John. The town's gone wild, I think. She speak of Abigail, and I thought she were a saint, to hear her. Abigail brings the other girls into the court, and where she walks the crowd will part like the sea for Israel. And folks are brought before them, and if they scream and howl and fall to the floor – the person's clapped in the jail for bewitchin' them.

**Proctor** *(wide-eyed)* Oh, it is a black mischief.

**Elizabeth** I think you must go to Salem, John. *(He turns to her)* I think so. You must tell them it is a fraud.

**Proctor** *(thinking beyond this)* Aye, it is, it is surely.

**Elizabeth** Let you go to Ezekiel Cheever – he knows you well. And tell him what she said to you last week in her uncle's house. She said it had naught to do with witchcraft, did she not?

**Proctor** *(in thought)* Aye, she did, she did. *(Now, a pause)*

**Elizabeth** *(quietly, fearing to anger him by prodding)* God forbid you keep that from the court, John. I think they must be told.

**Proctor** *(quietly, struggling with his thought)* Aye, they must, they must. It is a wonder they do believe her.

**Elizabeth** I would go to Salem now, John – let you go tonight.

**Proctor** I'll think on it.

**Elizabeth** *(with her courage now)* You cannot keep it, John.

**Proctor** *(angering)* I know I cannot keep it. I say I will think on it!

**Elizabeth** *(hurt, and very coldly)* Good, then, let you think on it. *(She stands and starts to walk out of the room.)*

**Proctor** I am only wondering how I may prove what she told me, Elizabeth. If the girl's a saint now, I think it is not easy to prove she's fraud, and the town gone so silly. She told it to me in a room alone – I have no proof for it.

**Elizabeth** You were alone with her?

**Proctor** *(stubbornly)* For a moment alone, aye.

**Elizabeth** Why, then, it is not as you told me.

**Proctor** *(his anger rising)* For a moment, I say. The others come in soon after.

**Elizabeth** *(Quietly – she has suddenly lost all faith in him.)* Do as you wish, then. *(She starts to turn.)*

**Proctor** Woman. *(She turns to him.)* I'll not have your suspicion any more.

**Elizabeth** *(a little loftily)* I have no –

**Proctor** I'll not have it!

**Elizabeth** Then let you not earn it.

**Proctor** *(with a violent undertone)* You doubt me yet?

**Elizabeth** *(with a smile, to keep her dignity)* John, if it were not Abigail that you must go to hurt, would you falter now? I think not.

**Proctor** Now look you –

**Elizabeth** I see what I see, John.

**Proctor** *(with solemn warning)* You will not judge me more, Elizabeth. I have good reason to think before I charge fraud on Abigail, and I will think on it. Let you look to your own improvement before you go to judge your husband any more. I have forgot Abigail, and –

**Elizabeth** And I.

**Proctor** Spare me! You forget nothin' and forgive nothin'. Learn charity, woman. I have gone tiptoe in this house all seven month since she is gone. I have not moved from there to there without I think to please you, and still an everlasting funeral marches round your heart. I cannot speak but I am doubted, every moment judged for lies, as though I come into a court when I come into this house!

**Elizabeth** John, you are not open with me. You saw her with a crowd, you said. Now you –

**Proctor** I'll plead my honesty no more, Elizabeth.

**Elizabeth** *(now she would justify herself)* John, I am only –

**Proctor** No more! I should have roared you down when first you told me your suspicion. But I wilted, and, like a Christian, I confessed. Confessed! Some dream I had must have mistaken you for God that day. But you're not, you're not, and let you remember it! Let you look sometimes for the goodness in me, and judge me not.

**Elizabeth**  I do not judge you. The magistrate sits in your heart that judges you. I never thought you but a good man, John – *(with a smile)* – only somewhat bewildered.

**Proctor** *(laughing bitterly)*  Oh, Elizabeth, your justice would freeze beer! *(He turns suddenly toward a sound outside. He starts for the door as Mary Warren enters. As soon as he sees her, he goes directly to her and grabs her by her cloak, furious.)* How do you go to Salem when I forbid it? Do you mock me? *(shaking her)* I'll whip you if you dare leave this house again!

*Strangely, she doesn't resist him, but hangs limply by his grip.*

**Mary Warren**  I am sick, I am sick, Mr Proctor. Pray, pray, hurt me not. *(Her strangeness throws him off, and her evident pallor and weakness. He frees her.)* My insides are all shuddery; I am in the proceedings all day, sir.

**Proctor** *(with draining anger – His curiosity is draining it.)*  And what of these proceedings here? When will you proceed to keep this house, as you are paid nine pound a year to do – and my wife not wholly well?

*As though to compensate,* **Mary Warren** *goes to* **Elizabeth** *with a small rag doll.*

**Mary Warren**  I made a gift for you today, Goody Proctor. I had to sit long hours in a chair, and passed the time with sewing.

**Elizabeth** *(perplexed, looking at the doll)*  Why, thank you, it's a fair poppet.

**Mary Warren** *(with a trembling, decayed voice)*  We must all love each other now, Goody Proctor.

**Elizabeth** *(amazed at her strangeness)*  Aye, indeed we must.

**Mary Warren** *(glancing at the room)*  I'll get up early in the morning and clean the house. I must sleep now. *(She turns and starts off.)*

**PROCTOR** Mary. *(She halts.)* Is it true? There be fourteen women arrested?

**MARY WARREN** No, sir. There be thirty-nine now – *(She suddenly breaks off and sobs and sits down, exhausted.)*

**ELIZABETH** Why, she's weepin'! What ails you, child?

**MARY WARREN** Goody Osburn – will hang! *(There is a shocked pause, while she sobs.)*

**PROCTOR** Hang! *(He calls into her face.)* Hang, y'say?

**MARY WARREN** *(through her weeping)* Aye.

**PROCTOR** The Deputy Governor will permit it?

**MARY WARREN** He sentenced her. He must. *(to ameliorate it)* But not Sarah Good. For Sarah Good confessed, y'see.

**PROCTOR** Confessed! To what?

**MARY WARREN** That she – *(in horror at the memory)* – she sometimes made a compact with Lucifer, and wrote her name in his black book – with her blood – and bound herself to torment Christians till God's thrown down – and we all must worship Hell forevermore.

*(Pause)*

**PROCTOR** But – surely you know what a jabberer she is. Did you tell them that?

**MARY WARREN** Mr Proctor, in open court she near to choked us all to death.

**PROCTOR** How, choked you?

**MARY WARREN** She sent her spirit out.

**ELIZABETH** Oh, Mary, Mary, surely you –

**MARY WARREN** *(with an indignant edge)* She tried to kill me many times, Goody Proctor!

**Elizabeth** Why, I never heard you mention that before.

**Mary Warren** I never knew it before. I never knew anything before. When she come into the court I say to myself, I must not accuse this woman, for she sleep in ditches, and so very old and poor. But then – then she sit there, denying and denying, and I feel a misty coldness climbin' up my back, and the skin on my skull begin to creep, and I feel a clamp around my neck and I cannot breathe air; and then – *(entranced)* – I hear a voice, a screamin' voice, and it were my voice – and all at once I remembered everything she done to me!

**Proctor** Why? What did she do to you?

**Mary Warren** *(like one awakened to a marvellous secret insight)* So many time, Mr Proctor, she come to this very door, beggin' bread and a cup of cider – and mark this: whenever I turned her away empty, she mumbled.

**Elizabeth** Mumbled! She may mumble if she's hungry.

**Mary Warren** But what does she mumble? You must remember, Goody Proctor. Last month – a Monday, I think – she walked away, and I thought my guts would burst for two days after. Do you remember it?

**Elizabeth** Why – I do, I think, but –

**Mary Warren** And so I told that to Judge Hathorne, and he asks her so. "Goody Osburn," says he, "what curse do you mumble that this girl must fall sick after turning you away?" And then she replies – *(mimicking an old crone)* – "Why, your excellence, no curse at all. I only say my commandments; I hope I may say my commandments," says she!

**Elizabeth** And that's an upright answer.

**Mary Warren** Aye, but then Judge Hawthorne say, "Recite for us your commandments!" – *(leaning avidly toward them)* – and of all the ten she could not say a single one. She never knew no commandments, and they had her in a flat lie!

**Proctor** And so condemned her?

**Mary Warren** *(now a little strained, seeing his stubborn doubt)* Why, they must when she condemned herself.

**Proctor** But the proof, the proof!

**Mary Warren** *(with greater impatience with him)* I told you the proof. It's hard proof, hard as rock, the judges said.

**Proctor** *(pauses an instant, then)* You will not go to court again, Mary Warren.

**Mary Warren** I must tell you, sir, I will be gone every day now. I am amazed you do not see what weighty work we do.

**Proctor** What work you do! It's strange work for a Christian girl to hang old women!

**Mary Warren** But, Mr Proctor, they will not hang them if they confess. Sarah Good will only sit in jail some time – *(recalling)* – and here's a wonder for you; think on this, Goody Good is pregnant!

**Elizabeth** Pregnant! Are they mad? The woman's near to sixty!

**Mary Warren** They had Doctor Griggs to examine her, and she's full to the brim. And smokin' a pipe all these years, and no husband either! But she's safe, thank God, for they'll not hurt the innocent child. But be that not a marvel? You must see it, sir, it's God's work we do. So I'll be gone every day for some time. I'm – I am an official of the court, they say, and I – *(She has been edging toward offstage.)*

**Proctor** I'll official you! *(He strides to the mantel, takes down the whip hanging there.)*

**Mary Warren** *(terrified, but coming erect, striving for her authority)* I'll not stand whipping any more!

**Elizabeth** *(hurriedly, as Proctor approaches)* Mary, promise now you'll stay at home –

**Mary Warren** *(backing from him, but keeping her erect posture, striving, striving for her way)* The Devil's loose in Salem, Mr Proctor; we must discover where he's hiding!

**Proctor** I'll whip the Devil out of you! *(With whip raised he reaches out for her, and she streaks away and yells.)*

**Mary Warren** *(pointing at Elizabeth)* I saved her life today! *(Silence. His whip comes down.)*

**Elizabeth** (softly) I am accused?

**Mary Warren** *(quaking)* Somewhat mentioned. But I said I never see no sign you ever sent your spirit out to hurt no one, and seeing I do live so closely with you, they dismissed it.

**Elizabeth** Who accused me?

**Mary Warren** I am bound by law, I cannot tell it. *(to Proctor)* I only hope you'll not be so sarcastical no more. Four judges and the King's deputy sat to dinner with us but an hour ago. I – I would have you speak civilly to me, from this out.

**Proctor** *(in horror, muttering in disgust at her)* Go to bed.

**Mary Warren** *(with a stamp of her foot)* I'll not be ordered to bed no more, Mr Proctor! I am eighteen and a woman, however single!

**Proctor** Do you wish to sit up? Then sit up.

**Mary Warren** I wish to go to bed!

**Proctor** *(in anger)* Good night.

*Dissatisfied, uncertain of herself, she goes out. Wide-eyed, both* **Proctor** *and* **Elizabeth** *stand staring.*

**Elizabeth** *(quietly)* Oh, the noose, the noose is up!

# *Staging the extract*

##  SET DESIGN

The play is specific to the period of 1692 and to the simple wooden dwellings built by the Puritan settlers of the time. The staging requirements for the extract include an exterior door and a staircase that leads to the bedrooms above. There is also mention of a fireplace and a washbasin that might be under an exterior window. The script suggests that the sets should be realistic and the original production on a proscenium arch stage was but it is possible to use minimal staging. This can be achieved by staging the extract in-the-round so that the atmosphere and sense of place are created mostly by the use of flooring, properties and lighting.

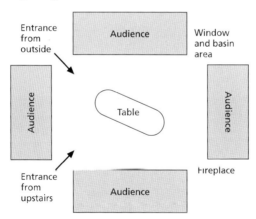

◆2a **Staging activity**

> Create the in-the-round setting illustrated above in your school studio by marking out the floor with tape. Experiment with different sizes and shapes of floor space and with the size of the table. Try the entrances, the fireplace, the table position and the washbasin in different places to see which combination is most effective.

**CAMPAIGNS AND CONFLICTS**

◆2b **Props activity**

H
- Go through the extract and make a list of furniture and props.
- Research each of the items from your list and find a visual image for each. Paste your images into a folder and label each one. You will find images in history books and on websites. You may also find items in museums that you may be able to photograph.
- Which of the props could be made? Which would have to be borrowed? Which would have to be bought?

## COSTUME

Costume design is restricted by the nature of Puritan dress, which was simple and plain. It is important to research the kind of clothes that were worn in the early to late 17th-century by working people. John and Elizabeth Proctor are farming people and Mary Warren is their maid, so they will be wearing clothes that are lived in and worked in. Such clothes would not be vastly different from those of the Puritans in 17th-century England.

*Judges who give no quarter in the witch-hunt trials ...*

**LIGHTING**

The lighting for the play needs to create a mood. In this extract the sources of light are:

- the night sky (possibly moonlight) coming through the outside door and the window
- the light of the fire from the fireplace
- candlelight.

The lighting needs to strike a balance between being low level and high enough to see the actors' faces. How might you create the appropriate atmosphere with the use of colour and shadows in your lighting design?

 **SOUND**

There is little mention of sound in the extract apart from that made by Mary Warren before she enters the room. However, sound can be used to create atmosphere and a sense of the outside world. There is the crackling of the fire within. Outside there might be the song of the crickets, the occasional hoot of an owl or dogs barking in the distance. Think of sound as aural scenery to create an atmosphere.

CAMPAIGNS AND CONFLICTS

# *Exploring the extract*

## HISTORICAL AND CULTURAL CONTEXT

*The Crucible* inhabits two almost parallel worlds:

- the historical world of Salem in the early 1690s when the witch-hunt hysteria destroyed innocent people and served to settle a few personal scores
- the real world of America in the early 1950s when Senator Joseph McCarthy set up the House Un-American Activities Committee and hounded anyone suspected of connections to communism.

Beyond these two specific contexts, the play explores the universal theme of playing on people's prejudices to attack a particular group considered to be undesirable by some.

◆2c **Research and discussion**

Investigate the communist "witch-hunts" in 1950s America engineered by Senator Joseph McCarthy. What happened to people named by the House Un-American Activities Committee?

Consider the relationship of these real-life events to those of *The Crucible*.

Research into 20th-century history for cases in which one group in a society is being hunted down and destroyed, such as the persecution of the Jews under Hitler, ethnic cleansing in Bosnia and Croatia, apartheid in South Africa. Why can these events be described as witch-hunts? Why do people in the community fear to speak out against what is happening?

# GENRE AND SUBJECT MATTER

*The Crucible* can be described as a historical drama that uses realism to engage an audience about events of the past. It is emotional involvement with the characters that draws the audience into the world of the play. The extract takes place in the actual time it takes to play the scene but the pace of the action constantly alters depending upon the emotional state of the characters.

### ◆2d  Units of action: directing

For the purpose of directing, the scene can be broken down into units of action that are defined by the changing motivation or mood of the characters. By identifying the units of action, you can work out changes of pace between each unit. Pace is achieved partly through the speed at which someone speaks and partly through the use of pauses within and between lines of dialogue. Units of action are very much a matter of interpretation and need to be worked out between the actors and the director. The following exercise provides a method for working out the pace best suited to the unit of action.

Look at the list of five different paces below. Then see how these are matched to the units of action suggested in the table.

---

Pace 1
The dialogue is spoken slowly with much use of pause and moments of stillness in which the characters take time to think about what they are saying.

---

Pace 2
The dialogue is spoken at a speed somewhere between that of ordinary speech and thoughtful speech.

---

Pace 3
The dialogue is spoken at the speed of ordinary speech. The character is steady in what they are saying.

---

Pace 4
The dialogue is spoken at a speed somewhere between ordinary speech and speech that is excited by emotions.

---

Pace 5
The dialogue is spoken quickly with much energy, force and passion. The character hardly has time to think about what they are saying.

**CAMPAIGNS AND CONFLICTS**

| Unit | From: | To: | Reason: | Pace: |
|---|---|---|---|---|
| 30 | 1. | **PROCTOR:** I think you're sad again. Are you? | **ELIZABETH:** Mary Warren's there today. | It has taken John a while to speak and to break the awkwardness between them. | 2 |
| 31 | 2. | **PROCTOR:** Why'd you let her? | **ELIZABETH:** … and says to me, 'I must go to Salem, Goody Proctor; I am an official of the court!' | John is suddenly angry with Elizabeth for allowing Mary Warren to disobey his order. | 4 |
| 31 | 3. | **PROCTOR:** Court! What court? | **ELIZABETH:**… the person's clapped in the jail for bewitchin' them, | This is the first that John has heard about the court and Elizabeth gives an explanation. | 3 |

Copy out the table and complete it for the next three units you decide upon and use the chart to mark the pace by number in the last column.

◆2e **Ancient or modern?**

One of the distinguishing features of The Crucible is the way in which Arthur Miller has created a dialect to give the impression of people living in the late 17th-century.

There is something about the following examples of dialogue that makes the language sound old-fashioned. Discuss in small groups what gives you the idea that the characters are speaking 17th-century English.

Identify other examples from the extract and provide an explanation for each.

There be fourteen people in the jail now, she says.

Aye, they must, they must. It is a wonder they do believe her.

I have good reason to think before I charge fraud on Abigail, and I will think on it.

I only hope you'll not be so sarcastical no more.

# *Exploring characters*

## JOHN PROCTOR

At the heart of the play is the consequence of the human failing in John Proctor. He has been unable to resist his sexual attraction to the teenage Abigail Warren and the feeling of lost trust between husband and wife runs throughout the extract. He is brusque and defensive, exploding in anger at Mary Warren as a release to his emotions.

### ♦2f Thoughts in the Head

*Organization:* This exercise requires at least three people, one to play the role of Elizabeth, one to play the role of John and one or more to play the role of Abigail as thoughts in John's head.

*Situation:* Elizabeth and John act out the section that starts with the line:

**ELIZABETH:** I think you must go to Salem, John.

and finishes with the line:

**PROCTOR:** I'll not have it.

> I'd almost forgotten how strong you are, John Proctor!
> Give me a word, John. A soft word.
> John – I am waitin' for you every night.
> I know how you clutched my back behind your house and sweated like a stallion whenever I came near!
> You're surely sportin' with me.
> I saw your face when she put me out, and you loved me then and you do now!
> I have a sense for heat, John, and yours has drawn me to my window.
> I have seen you looking up, burning in your loneliness.
> Do you tell me you've never looked up at my window?
> I look for John Proctor that took me from my sleep and put knowledge in my heart!

*cont...*

CAMPAIGNS AND CONFLICTS

> Look at Abigail's lines in Act One, above. In this exercise, these can be spoken in any order before one of John's lines in the extract. To start, play the scene through once and take note of the feelings and actions of John and Elizabeth. John has 10 lines to say in this sequence. Before he speaks each line, another actor is going to speak one of Abigail's lines as though they were thoughts in his head. Abigail can be on stage, unseen by Elizabeth, as though she is John's conscience, or the lines can be spoken from off stage.
>
> Play the scene a second time and notice the effect that the thoughts in the head have on John's feelings and actions. How does this alter the way the actor behaves and speaks? What does the exercise show you about John Proctor's character?

## ELIZABETH PROCTOR

Proctor says to Elizabeth in this extract, "You forget nothin' and forgive nothin'." Yet it is clear from her willingness to lie on his behalf in court later on, thinking to save his life, that she loves him and has probably forgiven his adultery. Then why is she so cold and forbidding in this scene?

### ◆2g **Role-play**

> *Organization:* Working in pairs, one person is going to role-play Elizabeth and the other John.
>
> *Situation:* It is seven months before the events in the extract. After supper, John and Elizabeth are sitting at the kitchen table. The children are in bed. Elizabeth feels that John is becoming a stranger to her. She has noticed that he spends a lot of time talking to their teenage servant, Abigail Warren.
>
> *Opening line:* **ELIZABETH:** John, you have been late out these past few evenings…

# MARY WARREN

Mary Warren is described as a "subservient, naïve, lonely girl". She is a dangerous character as far as John Proctor is concerned. She is frightened of both Abigail and of Proctor who have control over her at various times. Proctor describes Mary as a "mouse" in the extract, but she stands up to him this time. Mary is indeed weak-minded and goes with the side that she feels can offer her the best protection. This makes her a danger as she is unstable and easily manipulated. In the extract she brings Elizabeth the poppet in which Abigail has hidden a needle. This enables Abigail to accuse Elizabeth of being a witch when she pretends to be stabbed and testifies that "it were your wife's [Elizabeth's] familiar spirit pushed it in". Mary reveals that she has condemned Goody Osburn as a witch and, when Proctor thinks he can call on her to tell the court that Abigail is lying about being possessed by evil spirits, she is easily turned and condemns him as the "devil's man."

◆2h **Hot-seating**

*Organization:* One person is in character as Mary Warren and sits on a chair facing the rest of the group. Members of the group take it in turns to ask questions that are related to the play, which the person playing Mary Warren must answer in character.

**Sample questions:**
- Why did you go to Salem when John Proctor has forbidden you to go?
- How do you feel when John Proctor threatens to whip you?
- Why did you tell the court that Goody Osburn tried to kill you many times?
- What made you save Elizabeth's life in the court today?
- How do you like being an official of the court?

# COMPARING TEXTS

From "The Crucible: Guilt Tripping", a review by Lloyd Rose of the *Washington Post* of the 1996 film version.

*The Crucible* is a period piece, but the period isn't the 17th-century, it's the 1950s, with its sexual skittishness and out-of-control teenagers. The kitten-with-a-whip villainess, the pseudo-poetic dialogue, the melodramatic division of good folk vs. evil – all these bring the script to the verge of the ludicrous. But Hyntner (the film's director) treats it as if it were Shakespeare. He doesn't seem to understand that what he's directed could be subtitled, 'Blood-Crazed Teen Bimbos from Inner Space.'

### ◆2i Discussion and writing

What is this reviewer's attitude towards the film version of the play? How do his views compare with yours regarding the play and/or the film of the play?

### ◆2j Improvisation

**In groups**
The above review suggests a number of different genres, among them horror movies and melodrama. Using the situations and characters from the extract, improvise a scene working in a genre of your choice. (Science fiction, situation comedy, soap opera are some others.) How does the genre affect the way the ideas are communicated and the characters are portrayed?

EXTRACT 3

# Oh What a Lovely War
## Theatre Workshop and Charles Chilton

"This is not a conventional play and will not come to life if treated as such. It was first performed by a company of 15 skilled dancers and singers, accustomed to improvisation and guided by a director," wrote Joan Littlewood, the original director of the play and one of the founders of the Theatre Workshop. The show has no named playwright as the script was the result of an idea from Gerry Raffles (who had heard a BBC radio programme of songs from the World War I); a draft version of a script and with follow-up research by Charles Chilton; a plot outline by Joan Littlewood and the final version a collaboration between the director and the cast.

Joan Littlewood was born in 1914 in Stockwell, London, and was the daughter of an unwed housemaid. She trained at the Royal Academy of Dramatic Art as an actor but left without completing the course, which she felt led to a kind of theatre she was not interested in. She wanted to create shows that appealed to ordinary working class people. She worked as an assistant manager and actor in Manchester, joining a company called Theatre of Action in 1936. In 1945 along with Ewan McColl and Gerry Raffles she formed the Theatre Workshop and toured around village halls and community centres. In 1953 the company settled at the Theatre Royal in Stratford East, a working class district of London. In the 1950s the Theatre Workshop discovered and produced such plays as *The Quare Fellow* and *The Hostage* by Brendan Behan and *A Taste of Honey* by Shelagh Delaney. Joan Littlewood left the Theatre Workshop in 1961 to work abroad but was persuaded to come back in 1963 by Gerry Raffles to create *Oh What a Lovely War*. After the production's successful transfer to London's West End, Joan Littlewood never worked in the British theatre again.

## SUMMARY OF THE PLOT

*Oh What a Lovely War* is a retelling of the events of World War I through the songs of the period performed by a pierrot (clown) troupe playing *The War Game*. Pierrot shows were popular all over England in the 1890s and early 1900s, mostly at end of the pier theatres in seaside towns. Throughout the play, information is projected onto a screen as a newspanel starting with: "SUMMER 1914. SCORCHING BANK HOLIDAY FORECAST" and finishing with "THE WAR TO END WARS… KILLED TEN MILLION…WOUNDED TWENTY-ONE MILLION…MISSING SEVEN MILLION." Some scenes in between contrast the ridiculous decisions of governments and high ranking officers with the dire consequences for the working class soldiers on the battlefield. Others show the delight of war profiteers and the patriotic hysteria created by propaganda.

## THE SCENES IN CONTEXT

Because the play is structured like Music Hall turns (acts), there is no plot as such and each scene is complete in its own right. Act One covers the time just before the war breaks out in 1914 up until January 1915. Act Two covers the rest of the war. The two scenes in the extract are taken from the second half of the show and demonstrate the way in which each episode tells a full story but is linked to the next by the use of a particular piece of music.

# *Oh What a Lovely War*

By

## Theatre Workshop and Charles Chilton – UK

## CAST LIST

The play is written for a company of performers with each actor having a number of parts to play. This extract has been cast for eight players (4 male and 4 female) and the roles are distributed among them. The roles may be distributed differently and the size and gender of the cast altered to suit different groups.

**PLAYER 1** – First Man; M.C.; Fifth Soldier

**PLAYER 2** – First Girl; First Woman; Second Soldier

**PLAYER 3** – Second Girl; Second Woman; Third Soldier

**PLAYER 4** – Third Girl; Mrs Pankhurst; Fourth Soldier

**PLAYER 5** – Fourth Girl; First Soldier

**PLAYER 6** – Second Man; Haig

**PLAYER 7** – Third Man; British General

**PLAYER 8** – Fourth Man; Sergeant

All of the company play pierrots at the beginning and at the end of the extract.

## Setting

*The stage is set as for a pierrot show of the 1910s with red, white and blue fairy lights, twin balconies left and right and coloured circus 'tubs', which are used as seats and in other ways throughout the play. Above the stage there is a newspanel across which messages are flashed during the action. There is also a screen behind the acting area, onto which slides are projected. The numbers in the song lyrics indicate which slide is to be projected at a certain point in the song.*

# Newspanel

**NEWSPANEL 1915**  April 22 ... Battle of Ypres ... Germans use poison gas ... British loss 59,275 men ... May 9 ... Aubers Ridge ... British loss 11,619 men in 15 hours ... Last of BEF ... Gain nil... Sept 25 ... Loos ... British loss 8,236 men in 3 hours .. German loss nil.

*The company dressed as pierrots enter and sing.*

**SONG**  OH IT'S A LOVELY WAR
Oh, oh, oh, it's a lovely war,
Who wouldn't be a soldier, eh?
Oh, it's a shame to take the pay;
As soon as reveille is gone,
We feel just as heavy as lead,
But we never get up till the sergeant
Brings our breakfast up to bed.
Oh, oh, oh, it's a lovely war,
What do we want with eggs and ham,
When we've got plum and apple jam?
Form fours, right turn,
How shall we spend the money we earn?

Oh, oh, oh, it's a lovely war.
Up to your waist in water,
Up to your eyes in slush,
Using the kind of language,
That makes the sergeant blush.
Who wouldn't join the army?
That's what we all inquire;
Don't we pity the poor civilian,
Sitting beside the fire.

Oh, oh, oh, it's a lovely war,
Who wouldn't be a soldier, eh?
Oh, it's a shame to take the pay;
As soon as reveille is gone,
We feel just as heavy as lead,
But we never get up till the sergeant
Brings our breakfast up to bed.

> Oh, oh, oh, it's a lovely war,
> What do we want with eggs and ham,
> When we've got plum and apple jam?
> Form fours, right turn,
> How shall we spend the money we earn?
> Oh, oh, oh, it's a lovely war.

**1 M.C.** Ladies and gentlemen, when the Conscription Act was passed, 51,000 able-bodied men left home without leaving any forwarding addresses …

*6, 7, and 8 go off quickly.*

**2, 3, 4, 5 Girls** Shame!

**1 M.C.** … and that's in West Ham alone.

*As each of the girls speaks her line to the audience she throws a white feather.*

**2 First Girl** Women of England, do your duty, send your men to enlist today!

**3 Second Girl** Have you an able-bodied groom, chauffeur or gamekeeper serving you?

**4 Third Girl** If so, shouldn't he be serving his country?

**5 Fourth Girl** Is your best boy in khaki? If not shouldn't he be?

**2, 3, 4 & 5 Girls** What did you do in the Great War, Daddy?

**Girls** *(sing)*   Oh, oh, oh, it's a lovely,
             Oh, oh, oh, it's a lovely,
             Oh, oh, oh, it's a lovely war!

*The **M.C.** comes in and sets a stand for **Mrs Pankhurst**. During the following scene he wanders round the stage as a silent observer. **Mrs Pankhurst** and a crowd of bystanders come on. As she climbs on her box the crowd whistle.*

**1 First Man** Shut up!

**4 Mrs Pankhurst** Now, before talking to you all, I should like to read you a letter from my friend George Bernard Shaw.

**6 Second Man** Who's he when he's at home?

**2 First Woman** Ain't it disgusting?

**4 Mrs Pankhurst** He says: 'The men of this country are being sacrificed to the blunders of boobies, the cupidity of capitalists, the ambition of conquerors, the lusts and lies and rancours of bloodthirsts that love war, because it opens their prison doors and sets them on the throne of power and popularity.'

**7 Third Man** Now give us a song!

**4 Mrs Pankhurst** For the second time peace is being offered to the sorely tried people of the civilized world …

**6 Second Man** Hallo.

**4 Mrs Pankhurst** … at the close of 1915 President Wilson proposed an immediate armistice; to be followed by a peace conference …

**6 Second Man** Hallo!

**4 Mrs Pankhurst** … in April of this year, Germany herself proposed peace …

**6 Second Man** Hallo! Hallo!

**4 Mrs Pankhurst** … the peace movements are strong in England, France and the United States; and in Germany. In the Reichstag …

**6 Second Man** Who's he when he's at home?

**4 Mrs Pankhurst** … the peace groups are active and outspoken; the exact terms of Germany's offer have never been made known to us and I should like to ask Lloyd George what his war aims are.

**2 First Woman** I should like to ask you what your old man has for dinner!

**4 Mrs Pankhurst** … the politicians chatter like imbeciles while civilization bleeds to death.

**7 Third Man** You're talking like a traitor. Pacifists are traitors.

**4 Mrs Pankhurst** I ask that gentleman …

**7 Third Man** Don't ask me … 'Cos I don't know nothing … I'm stupid.

**4 Mrs Pankhurst** … to consider the plight of the civilized world after another year: you do not know what you do and the statesmen wash their hands of the whole affair …

**8 Fourth Man** Why don't you wash your face!

**6 Second Man** Douglas Haig's got them on the run.

**4 Mrs Pankhurst** Who tells you this? The Times …

**6 Second Man** He's got them going.

**4 Mrs Pankhurst** … the newspaper that refuses to publish the pacifist letters, and distorts the facts of our so-called victories. We are killing off slowly but surely the best of the male population …

**2 First Woman** Here! Don't you address them words to me …

**3 Second Woman** Here! Don't you address them words to her …

**4 Mrs Pankhurst** … the sons of Europe are being crucified …

**2 First Woman** … my old man's at the front …

**3 Second Woman** She's had her share of suffering …

**4 Mrs Pankhurst** … on the barbed wire, because you …

**2 First Woman** Here, don't you address them words to me; my old man's at the front.

**4 Mrs Pankhurst** … you the misguided masses are crying out for it.

**3 Second Woman** Her old man's at the front.

**2 First Woman** My old man's at the front.

**4 Mrs Pankhurst** War cannot be won. No one can win a war. Is it your wish this war will go on and on until Germany is beaten to the ground?

**Newspanel** July 1 …. Somme ….. British loss 60,000 men on the first day.

**Crowd** Yes! Yes!

*They drown her with shouts. They sing.*

**Song** RULE, BRITANNIA
Rule, Britannia, Britannia rules the waves,
Britons, never, never, never shall be slaves.
Rule, Britannia, Britannia rules the waves,
Britons never, never, never shall …

# Whizzbang

*Men's voices offstage sing 'Hush, here comes a Whizzbang': a sequence of slides is projected as follows:*

*Slide 33: Night photographs of flares, and various Very lights.*

*Slide 34: Photograph of a cloud formation.*

*Slide 35: Three Tommies walking across duckboards in a muddy field.*

*Slide 36: Dead Germans lying in a shallow trench in a peaceful-looking country field.*

*Slide 37: A young French soldier, obviously on burial duty, laden with wooden crosses.*

*Slide 38: Dead French Poilus; one of them has a smile on his face.*

*Slide 39: A field with nothing but white wooden crosses as far as one can see.*

**Song** HUSH, HERE COMES A WHIZZBANG
(Tune: 'Hush, here comes the Dream Man')
(33) Hush, here comes a whizzbang, (34)
Hush, here comes a whizzbang, (35)
Now, you soldier men, get down those stairs, (36)
Down in your dugouts and say your prayers. (37)
Hush, here comes a whizzbang,
And it's making (38) straight for you,
And you'll see all the wonders (39) of no-man's-land,
If a whizzbang hits you.

**6 HAIG** *(entering)* Germany has shot her bolt. The prospects for 1916 are excellent.

**7 BRITISH GENERAL** *(entering)* Permission to speak, sir.

**6 HAIG** Of course.

*Slide 40: A map of Ypres and the surrounding district, showing Kitchener's Wood, Hill 60, Passchendaele, etc.*

**7 BRITISH GENERAL** If we continue in this way, the line of trenches will stretch from Switzerland to the sea. Neither we nor the Germans will be able to break through. The war will end in complete stalemate.

**6 HAIG** Nonsense. We need only one more big offensive to break through and win. My troops are of fine quality, and specially trained for this type of war.

**7 BRITISH GENERAL** This is not war, sir, it is slaughter.

**6 HAIG** God is with us. It is for King and Empire.

**7 BRITISH GENERAL** We are sacrificing lives at the rate of five to sometimes fifty thousand a day.

**6 HAIG** One battle, our superior morale, bombardment.

**7 BRITISH GENERAL** We are rather short of men, sir.

**6 HAIG** What's left?

**7 BRITISH GENERAL** The new chappies from Ireland have just arrived.

**6 HAIG** Rather wild untrained lot! Still, they'll be rearing to have a crack at the Bosche, and what they lack in training, they'll make up for in gallantry.

**7 BRITISH GENERAL** They've just got off the train. Most of them haven't eaten for forty-eight hours –

**6 HAIG** They are moving against a weakened and demoralized enemy. Capture the German line, without further delay.

*Six Irish soldiers, wearing green kilts and carrying rifles, enter and stand upstage of **Haig** and the **British General**. One soldier is carrying a Union Jack on a pole.*

**8 Sergeant**  Right boys, up and at 'em!

**1, 2, 3, 4, 5 All**  Up the Irish!

**Band**  IRISH WASHERWOMAN

*They dance an attack under bombardment as an Irish jig. They reach their objective and fling themselves down. Birdsong.*

**8 Sergeant**  We made it.

**5 First Soldier**  Where are we, Serg?

**8 Sergeant**  I reckon we've broken into a lull!

**2 Second Soldier**  It's nice, ain't it?

**3 Third Soldier**  Peaceful!

**5 First Soldier**  Ah, lovely! Look at that.

**4 Fourth Soldier**  Aye, Serg, look at that dirty great black mound of earth.

**8 Sergeant**  That's nothing … it's an earthwork. We're too near for guns the size o' that to get us. *(sniper's bullet)*

**3 Third Soldier**  What was that?

**8 Sergeant**  That must have been a stray one. I should keep under cover if I was you. Trouble is we've been fighting too well. We've arrived ahead of ourselves.

**2 Second Soldier**  Serg, how many trenches did we capture?

**8 Sergeant**  I reckon about nine.

**5 First Soldier**  No, ten.

**8 Sergeant**  Make it a round dozen – we'll all be mentioned in despatches for this, you know.

**2 SECOND SOLDIER** Will we be heroes, Serg?

**4 FOURTH SOLDIER** Ah sure, it'll be a great victory for the boys.

*Birdsong still continuing.*

**5 FIRST SOLDIER** What's that, Serg?

**8 SERGEANT** What's what?

**5 FIRST SOLDIER** Sounds like someone talking over there.

**3 THIRD SOLDIER** Look. It's some Limey wounded in that shell 'ole over there.

**8 SERGEANT** Where?

**3 THIRD SOLDIER** Look! Under that ridge.

**8 SERGEANT** You can't tell the quick from the dead, can you!

**4 FOURTH SOLDIER** They must have fallen in the last attack.

**2 SECOND SOLDIER** What are they blabbering about?

**8 SERGEANT** "Go back. Go back – you bloody fools". He's telling us to go back. Thanks, mush.

**5 FIRST SOLDIER** Jesus! That's easier said than done. Eh? You what? He says we're drawing their fire, and to get the flag down. *(bullet shot)*

**8 SERGEANT** Seamus, get that flag down.

**2 SECOND SOLDIER** Hey Serg – where did that last one come from?

**8 SERGEANT** I think it must have been our boys!

*All but the **Sergeant** get up and shout upstage.*

**ALL** Hey, don't shoot. It's us.

**2 SECOND SOLDIER** There's human beings over here.

*Heavy gun shell. They all flatten the ground.*

**8 Sergeant**  Now you see what you've done. You bloody idiots. Seamus!

**1 Fifth Soldier**  Serg?

**8 Sergeant**  You're the quickest on your pins. Report back to H.Q. pronto. Tell the artillery not to waste their shells on us, but to save them for Jerry. Tell them to raise their bloody sights a bit.

**1 Fifth Soldier**  Back through all that?

**8 Sergeant**  Yeah.

**1 Fifth Soldier**  On me own?

**8 Sergeant**  Now is it for us to all give ground when we've come so near the prize?

**1 Fifth Soldier**  No, I see that. I'll tell 'em the battle's been won.

**8 Sergeant**  Do that.

*1 **Fifth soldier** walks upstage.*

**1 Fifth Soldier**  Hey Serg, that last one got the bridge.

**2 Second Soldier**  Does that mean we're cut off then?

**1 Fifth Soldier**  No, I'll swim for it.

**8 Sergeant**  Give yourself a treat. That'll be the first wash he's had this year. Hey, Seamus, bring us back a bottle of whiskey – Irish! *(bullet shot)*

**2 Second Soldier**  He's gone under, Serg.

**8 Sergeant**  What do you mean?

**2 Second Soldier**  They got him.

**8 Sergeant**  Well, who's next? Come on, someone's got to go.

**4 Fourth Soldier**  I wouldn't mind a swim, Serg.

**8 Sergeant**  Right then, off you go. Tell them there's hundreds stranded on this ridge …

**2, 3, 5 ALL** Watch yourself, Jacko …

**4 FOURTH SOLDIER** Just watch me do the 100 yards in …

*He runs off – bullet gets him.*

**8 SERGEANT** Now if he's been shot, I'll kill him.

**2 SECOND SOLDIER** He has, Serg.

**8 SERGEANT** Well – I reckon we all better stick together.

*Heavy gun.*

They've started shelling for the next attack.

**2, 3, 5 ALL** Who?

**8 SERGEANT** The bloody mad English. Come on, let's get the hell out of here.

**2 SECOND SOLDIER** Where shall we go?

**8 SERGEANT** That's the question.

*Heavy gun and explosion.*

**2, 3, 5 ALL** *(shouting)* It's us. Stop shooting. It's us.

*Bullet shot. They all turn and face downstage.*

Kamerad – Kamerad …

*'Ping' from the band. They freeze, then reel off as if in a dream.*

**8 SERGEANT** This is it.

*Ping.*

**2 SECOND SOLDIER** Is it, Serg?

**3 THIRD SOLDIER** It's not so bad.

**5 First Soldier** No.

*Ping.*

**8 Sergeant** We've escaped the whole blooming war now.

**2 Second Soldier** I'll see ya, Serg.

**8 Sergeant** See ya.

*They go off. Full company enters for a song.*

*Slide Sequence*

*Slide 42: A group of eight or nine Highland infantrymen, around a small camp fire.*

*Slide 48: Canadian infantrymen in trench. One fast asleep, another writing home.*

*Slide 31: Four Tommies sitting in dugouts, which are merely holes, waist deep in mud.*

*Slide 49: Five Tommies trying to pull a field gun out of the mud.*

*Slide 50: A company of French Poilus marching past with rifles at the slope.*

*Slide 51: Two weary British officers, both in battle dress, one with bandaged head.*

*Slide 52: Two young Canadian soldiers, leaning against spiked boards, one writing a letter.*

*Slide 53: A long line of Tommies walking away from the camera, following the direction of a trench.*

> **Song**   AND WHEN THEY ASK US
> (Tune: 'They wouldn't believe me')
> (42) And when they ask us, how dangerous it was, (48)
> Oh, we'll never tell them, no, we'll never tell them: (31)
> We spent our pay in some café, (49)
> And fought wild women night and day,
> 'Twas the cushiest job we ever had. (50)
> And when they ask us, and they're certainly going to ask us, (51)

> The reason why we didn't win the Croix de Guerre, (52)
> Oh, we'll never tell them, oh, we'll never tell them (53)
> There was a front, but damned if we knew where.

FINALE  OH IT'S A LOVELY WAR
> Oh, oh, oh, it's a lovely war,
> What do we want with eggs and ham,
> When we've got plum and apple jam?
> Form fours, right turn,
> How shall we spend the money we earn?
> Oh, oh, oh, it's a lovely,
> Oh, oh, oh, it's a lovely,
> Oh, oh, oh, it's a lovely war!

# *Staging the extract*

##  SET DESIGN

The stage for *Oh What a Lovely War* is bare and needs little scenery apart from the following that Joan Littlewood considered essential for the play:

> A large screen, flown in and out, behind the acting area, on which slides of photographs of that war were projected to counterpoint the words of the songs.

> A newspanel which traversed the stage on which the names of battles appeared, followed by the number of those killed and wounded and the number of yards gained or lost.

> The pierrots, the screen and the newspanel must all be in the same field of vision. If either the newpanel or the screen is suspended elsewhere, at the side of the auditorium for example, the audience will simply not look at them.

> The only furniture: four truncated cones used as seats.

##  COSTUMES

All the male members of the cast are dressed as pierrots in white satin suits with black bobbles and ruffs and pointed hats. The women wear crinolines and long black lace stockings. Joan Littlewood would have no khaki on the stage, saying, "Even the word makes you think of war." To suggest different army ranks and regiments of soldiers, the actors change their pierrot hats for helmets and attach medals and stripes with Velcro. In the extract, for instance, Haig and the General need to wear something to show that they are officers. The Irish Soldiers wear green kilts instead of trousers. The women change their hats and wear shawls and scarves for different characters.

**Oh What a Lovely War**

*An actor adds jacket and hat as another character*

◆3a **Costume plot**

Even within the extract, each actor plays at least two different roles. It is therefore essential to track the costume changes that occur during the performance and to plan for them. Prepare your own costume plot for the extract using the following as a template.

Draw three columns on a sheet of paper using the following headings:

| Actor's Name | Roles Played | Costumes needed |
|---|---|---|
|  |  |  |
|  |  |  |
|  |  |  |

Complete each column to track the requirements for costume changes.

H

##  LIGHTING

Lighting is crucial in this extract to suggest the changes of location. The lighting design also has to incorporate the use of the projection screen as much as possible. It is also suggested in the script that little red and blue light bulbs be used around the set as for a seaside show. The

**65**

## CAMPAIGNS AND CONFLICTS

lighting must make a clear contrast between the song-and-dance narratives and the battlefield scenes.

### ♦3b Lighting plot

**H** Make a list of the lighting requirements for this extract, starting:
1. Lighting for song: *Oh, it's a lovely war*
2. Follow spot on MC
3. Lighting change for "Women of England" section.

##  SOUND EFFECTS

The following sounds are mentioned in the extract:
- Birdsong
- Sniper's bullet
- Birdsong still continuing
- Bullet shots (three times)
- Heavy gun shell
- Heavy gun
- Heavy gun and explosion

### ♦3c Sound tape

Go through the script and identify where each of the sound effects occurs. Produce a sound plot using the following template:

| Cue No: | Actual Cue Line for effect: | Sound Effect (Description) | Approximate length of sound cue (in seconds) | Sound source (eg title of CD) |
|---|---|---|---|---|
|  |  |  |  |  |

Research recordings for each of the sound effects. It is important that the gunfire and explosions are appropriate for weapons that were used during World War I.

Work out the approximate timings for each of the sound effects. It will help if you can attend rehearsals with a stopwatch. You will need to work out with the cast the length of each of the explosions. Judging the length of the birdsong is difficult because other sounds have to be heard at the same time and the actors may not always play the scene at the same speed in performance. It is worth considering playing the birdsong continuously on one playback system of tape recorder or CD player and playing the other effect on a second playback system. The sounds can then be mixed and cued live.

Make your sound tape and try it out in rehearsal with actors speaking the lines.

## MUSIC AND SONGS

Songs are an integral part of the play. All of the songs were written before or during World War I. Some are a parody of existing songs. For example, *Hush, here comes a whizzbang* is set to the tune of *Hush, here comes the dream man*.

These are the music requirements of the extract:

1  *Oh, it's a lovely war*
2  Reprise of the chorus of *Oh, it's a lovely war*
3  *Rule Britannia*
4  *Hush, here comes a whizzbang*
5  Irish jig, *The Irish Washer Woman*
6  Three pings made by the band. Actors are moving in slow motion when they are dead, so the pings could suggest an eerie dream-like state. This could be created by using brushes on cymbals or shaking a bell-tree.
7  *And when they ask us*
8  Reprise of *Oh, it's a lovely war*

The cast will need to know the songs thoroughly. While it adds to the effect if live musical accompaniment is used, for example, piano and drums, this is not absolutely necessary.

## DANCE AND MOVEMENT

There is a need to choreograph the musical numbers, particularly the opening song when the full company comes on stage. There is also an interesting moment when the Irish soldiers have to "dance an attack under bombardment as an Irish jig." This requires the performers to learn a traditional Irish jig and then to find a way of distorting the dance so that it looks as though they are under fire.

*Oh What a Lovely War*

# *Exploring the extract*

## HISTORICAL AND CULTURAL CONTEXT

*Oh What a Lovely War* is a protest against war, based on World War I which was supposed to be "the war to end all wars". It wiped out a generation of young men through death and disability. During the period leading up to the war, there were enormous differences between the social classes in Great Britain. This is shown in the play by the great divide between the Officers, drawn from the upper classes, and the working class soldiers who became gun fodder. Another important factor that comes across in the extract is that women were treated as second class citizens, not even having the right to vote. A great amount of research about World War I was carried out by the original cast and much of this information was used in the final script.

♦3d **Research and Writing**

A good starting point to research material for this period is to look at the following website: www.firstworldwar.com

You will need to know something about the events and the historical figures that are portrayed in the extract. To help in this, it is useful to create an 'Archive Notice Board' that you can refer to in rehearsals. Each person in your group should investigate one or more of the research topics listed below. The results of the research should be recorded as a series of points on a sheet of A4 paper. Original images, maps or posters can also be put on the Archive Notice Board to form a visual collage.

### Research Topics

| Events: | People: | Places: |
|---|---|---|
| Battle of Ypres (April 1915) | BEF (British Expeditionary Force) | Ypres |
| Conscription Act | Mrs Pankhurst | Aubers Bridge |
| Battle of the Somme | George Bernard Shaw | Loos |
| | President Wilson | Reichstag |
| | Lloyd George | |
| | Sir Douglas Haig | |
| | Bosche | |

**69**

## ♦3e Key Questions

Find out the information that will help you to answer and discuss the following questions:

- What event started World War I?
- Why was Britain at war with Germany?
- What was gained by the loss of so many lives in World War I?

# GENRE AND SUBJECT MATTER

In broad terms, *Oh What a Lovely War* is a musical play. It deliberately attempts to present the serious subject of war as comedy through a series of acts in the style of an end of the pier seaside show. The theatre in which the play was created was originally a Music Hall for popular entertainment and *Oh What a Lovely War* is intended to appeal to audiences that might not ordinarily go to the theatre. The audience is told about the horrifying number of deaths through the use of statistics on the newspanel. The Irish soldiers in the extract are shot and killed but they dance off the stage in a dream and are still speaking dialogue as though they are ghosts.

The play is both serious and funny at the same time. Much of the humour is conveyed through the new words of old songs. For instance, the soldiers sing *God Rest Ye Merry Gentlemen* with words of their own, and the rhyming word is left for the audience to supply:

> It was Christmas day in the cook 'ouse,
> The 'appiest day of the year,
> Men's 'earts were full of gladness
> And their bellies full of beer,
> When up spoke Private Short'ouse,
> His face as bold as brass
> Saying, "We don't want your Christmas puddin'
> You can stick it up your ..."
> Chorus: Tidings of comfort and joy, etc.

# Oh What a Lovely War

### ◆3f Discussion

> The subject of the play is the senseless horror of war. How is it possible to present this subject as entertainment? What is the effect of combining song and dance with scenes on the battlefield?

## BRECHT'S INFLUENCE ON THE PLAY

Joan Littlewood was very familiar with the plays and ideas of the German playwright and director, Bertolt Brecht. She uses a number of techniques influenced by him to create an *alienation* or *distancing* effect so that the audience does not get too emotionally involved in the play.

Performance and production are designed to ensure that the audience is always aware they are watching actors taking on the roles of different historical figures. The device of having the actors putting on a show called *The War Game* is in itself is a distancing effect. The use of slide projections, the newspanel and the songs all help the audience keep an emotional distance from the horrors described. This enables the audience to judge the events critically and cooly.

### ◆3g Alienation

> Go through the extract and identify all of the moments that help to create alienation. Explain why you think these are examples of *alienation*.
> Why is *alienation* used at the moments you have identified?
> Discuss your findings with other members of your group.

CAMPAIGNS AND CONFLICTS

# *Exploring characters*

It is difficult to explore character in this play because the characters are portraits or representations of historical figures and the roles were originally developed through improvisation. This is the general advice that Joan Littlewood gave to performers of the play:

> Play in the present tense. Avoid disclaiming. Cut emotion. Find the action in the speech. Throw out your ad-libs [off-the-cuff remarks] after one usage. However good they were, there are plenty more where they came from. Don't slow down.

In other words, it is important to keep the acting fresh, lively and energetic and to make the lines sound as if they are being improvised on the spot.

## MRS PANKHURST

The performer playing this role is making a speech about peace. It takes place in front of an audience of bystanders who believe that the war is justified and whose loved ones are fighting at the front. Her advocacy of peace does not make her popular.

### ♦3h Soapbox exercise

*Organization:* One person learns the dialogue spoken by **Mrs Pankhurst** as a continuous speech. Everyone else in the group is a Bystander who has someone close to them in battle. Some of the Bystanders will also know someone who has been killed in the war.

*Situation:* **Mrs Pankhurst** begins her speech to the crowd. Anyone from the crowd can call out a remark in response to what she is saying, but they must be **listening** to her words. **Mrs Pankhurst** can choose to carry on with her speech or respond to what is being said.

*Development:* Organize and rehearse the scene so that you can work out an order in which the Bystanders shout out. Rehearse the scene again to find ways of increasing the volume of each shouted line to eventually drown out **Mrs Pankhurst's** speech by singing *Rule Britannia*.

## ◆3i Thought-tracking

This exercise is about each Bystander finding an attitude towards Mrs Pankhurst. Remember that each Bystander knows someone who is risking their life at the front.

*Organization:* Play the scene with **Mrs Pankhurst** and the Bystanders again. This time, one person is going to be a *thought controller* with a whistle.

*Situation:* While the scene is being played, the *thought controller* blows the whistle at some point and everyone freezes. The *thought controller* taps some of the Bystanders on the shoulder and they have to speak out their thoughts about what **Mrs Pankhurst** is saying at that moment. The whistle blows and the scene continues until it is blown again.

# SIR DOUGLAS HAIG

## Sir Douglas Haig and The British General

This scene in the extract shows how out of touch Sir Douglas Haig, the commander in chief, is with what is going on at the front. The British General is trying to tell Haig that the situation is hopeless but he is not listening.

## ◆3j Nonsense exercise

*Organization:* Person A plays Haig and acts out the dialogue as written. Person B plays The British General but, after speaking the line, "Permission to speak, sir," replaces the given dialogue with nonsense – the more nonsensical the better.

*Situation:* Person B must try hard to get the full attention of Person A but Person A must try just as hard NOT to listen and continue speaking the lines as written.

Repeat the exercise a few times with Person B speaking as much nonsense as possible. Then play the scene with Person B speaking The British General's lines as written.

How does this exercise help the actor playing Haig to create a sense of character? How does it make the British General behave and feel towards Haig?

CAMPAIGNS AND CONFLICTS

# COMPARING TEXTS

### Blighters

by Siegfried Sassoon

The House is crammed: tier beyond tier they grin
And cackle at the Show, while prancing ranks
Of harlots shrill the chorus, drunk with din;
"We're sure the Kaiser loves our dear old Tanks!"

I'd like to see a Tank come down the stalls
Lurching to rag-time tunes, or "Home, sweet Home",
And there'd be no more jokes in Music-halls
To mock the riddled corpses round Bapaume.

♦3k **Discussion**

> Both the poem and the play use the metaphor of the theatre to contrast with War.
>
> Go through the poem and underline the words that are associated with the theatre. For example, "The House" at the beginning is a theatrical term to mean the audience.
>
> How does Sassoon's use of the theatre in his poem differ from the way it is used in the play?

### Bombardment

by Richard Aldington

Four days the earth was rent and torn
By bursting steel,
The houses fell about us;
Three nights we dared not sleep,
Sweating, and listening for the imminent crash
Which meant our death.

# Oh What a Lovely War

> The fourth night every man,
> Nerve-tortured, racked to exhaustion,
> Slept, muttering and twitching,
> While the shells crashed over head.
>
> The fifth day there came a hush;
> We left our holes
> And looked above the wreckage of the earth
> To where the white clouds moved in silent lines
> Across the untroubled blue.

## ◆3l Writing and discussion

Use the poem as a starting point to devise a scene that shows the effects of bombardment on a group of soldiers. Try to create the transition from noise and terror to silence and observation of a battered landscape. You can use lines and phrases from the poem, still-images and live or recorded sounds to create your interpretation.

How does the poem differ in its treatment of bombardment from that of the Irish Soldier scene in the extract?

## ◆3m Choral speaking

Choose one of the poems and reread it.

- Divide up the lines so that the poem can be spoken by a number of people. Experiment with having different numbers of speakers for some lines or even words. Be careful to consider the blend of the different types of voices in your group and the pace and volume the speakers use.
- Arrange the speakers so that they form a tableau or freeze-frame of soldiers under bombardment.
- As the poem proceeds, individuals might turn their backs or leave the tableau to represent soldiers being killed or wounded.

75

# Stronger than Superman
## Roy Kift

### ROY KIFT

Roy Kift was born in 1943 at Bideford in Devon. He trained as an actor but became a full-time playwright in 1972. He has lived in Germany since 1981, currently near Dortmund. Roy Kift has written over 20 plays, the best known of which is *Stronger than Superman*. Premiered in Berlin at the GRIPS Theatre in 1981, it has been translated and performed on stage in over 20 countries from Iceland to New Zealand and is still in repertoire in German theatres. Among his latest plays is *Camp Comedy* (premiered in New York, March 2003). This deals with the fate of the Jewish German actor and director Kurt Gerron who sang Mack the Knife in the first performance of Brecht and Weill's *Threepenny Opera*. Roy Kift also works as a translator.

### SUMMARY OF THE PLOT

*Stronger than Superman* tells the story of Chris, a young boy who uses a wheelchair. At the beginning of the play, Chris and his sister Paula have just moved to a new area and he is worried that he will not be able to stay with his mother and sister. Chris and Paula are playing together at home and this quickly establishes the fact that Chris's disability is a natural part of their everyday lives. Chris is threatened with being sent to a special home and finds an ally in a local charity worker, Mr Wright, who is also in a wheelchair. The scene ends with a song with a message about how people react to disabled people, sung by Chris and Mr Wright:

When a person's in a chair/It's obvious he's not all there!
Can't do nothing on his own/Best thing's put him in a home!
There's many many things that I can do/And many many things I can't
But what I really hate is when/You don't give me the chance.

In the following extract, Chris and Paula meet a local boy called Kevin who soon learns that being a wheelchair user does not make Chris so different from himself.

In the second half of the play, Kevin becomes a close friend of Chris and Paula and the audience learns more about Chris's disability as Kevin finds out about using callipers and everyday life as a wheelchair user. The play ends with the hope that the head teacher of Kevin's school can be persuaded to accept Chris and allow a "wheel-person" to be integrated with the "leg-people".

## THE SCENE IN CONTEXT

This is the scene when Chris and Paula meet Kevin for the first time.

# *Stronger than Superman*

By
Roy Kift – Germany/UK

## CAST LIST

**Mr Moody** – a security guard
**Kevin** – a boy of about ten
**Paula** – a girl of about nine (Chris's sister)
**Chris** – a boy of about ten
**Time:** the present
**Place:** the town in which the play is presented

*Most of the stage is taken up by a patch of private building land. This is fenced off from the narrow public footpath with a wire fence and warning notices. However, one part of the fence has been broken away, enabling children to get onto the land and play. Here we see **Kevin**, who is trying without much success to do tricks with a football. **Mr Moody**, a security guard, arrives. He is chewing a sweet.*

**Moody** Here, you!

**Kevin** What?

**Moody** Off! This is a demolition site, not a playground.

**Kevin** Where am I supposed to play then? On the ring-road?

**Moody** Less of the lip! Off! *(Kevin makes to go.)* I'm only saying for your own safety. Dangerous, see!

**Kevin** What they demolishing?

**Moody** Nothing. That's finished.

**KEVIN** What's dangerous then?

**MOODY** They're building.

**KEVIN** Where?

**MOODY** They're going to be building. Off!

**KEVIN** It's been like this for months!

**MOODY** And very soon men are going to be building here.

**KEVIN** Can't I play on it till they – ?

**MOODY** No, you can't! I said it's dangerous!

**KEVIN** What's the danger?

**MOODY** It's private property! Off!

**KEVIN** *(Goes towards the fence, then stops.)* What they going to build here?

**MOODY** Car park. Off!

**KEVIN** Why not a playground?

**MOODY** Look, working adults need somewhere to park their cars!

**KEVIN** Look, working children need somewhere to play after school!

**MOODY** All right clever, come here … Come here! … If you're so clever, come here! *(Kevin comes over.)* Take a look round. What do you see?

**KEVIN** Nothing.

**MOODY** A great patch of nothing. And that is valuable!

**KEVIN** Nothing is valuable?

**MOODY** *(stamping on the ground)* It's called land. Might look like nothing to you, but land is money. And the people who own this land want to get their money back quick!

**KEVIN** What for?

**Moody**  To buy more land, of course.

**Kevin**  What for?

**Moody**  To make more money, of course!

**Kevin**  What for?

**Moody**  To buy more land, of course!

**Kevin**  What for?

**Moody**  To make more money, of course! And they ain't going to get it from building playgrounds, are they? Ain't going to get it from your pocket-money! Now, off! And if I see you once more back on here, I'm calling the police. Understood?

*Kevin is about to go through the fence when the security guard pulls him back. He has seen **Chris** in his wheelchair.*

**Kevin**  Here! What are you doing?

*Moody nudges Kevin.*

**Moody**  *(secretively)*  There!

**Kevin**  What?

*Chris enters in his wheelchair. **Kevin** gapes.*

**Moody**  *(whispering)*  Poor kid! Spastic!

**Kevin**  Yeah?

**Moody**  Bit … *(He makes a sign to indicate that **Chris** is mental.)* … You know!

*(**Kevin** gapes. **Chris** becomes aware that he is being stared at. He glances over. **Kevin** and **Moody** look away.)*

**Moody**  *(loudly)*  Yeah, well, er, you heard what I said! Private! *(**Chris** looks away. **Moody** and **Kevin** stare back at him.)* Sad, really. Should be put away.

**Kevin** Killed?

**Moody** Wouldn't go that far. I mean, they're no use to no-one really, are they? I mean, never be able to work or nothing.

*Chris looks up again.* **Moody** *raises his hand in the air and gives a big smile, nods and waves. He nudges* **Kevin** *to do the same. The two of them wave, nod and smile like glazed puppets.* **Moody** *walks over to* **Chris** *awkwardly and drops a couple of sweets through the fence onto his lap.* **Chris** *stares at them for a moment, then wheels off.*

**Moody** Phew! *(to* **Kevin***)* Thank your lucky stars you're not a bit … *(He grunts like a mental defective, and begins to nod like a spastic.)* Ugh, ugh, ugh! *(in a deep nutty voice)* Give us an ice-cream, Mister! *(He pretends to take the cornet.)* Ta! *(He wobbles with the cornet before his mouth, then suddenly plops it in his eye. They both laugh)* Well, you got to, haven't yer? What's life without a larf? *(suddenly threatening)* And remember … Police!

*He watches* **Kevin** *go through the fence to the other side, then goes.* **Kevin** *does a few grunts to himself and imitates the ice-cream joke. He laughs to himself.* **Paula** *comes on. She looks round for* **Chris***, then walks through the broken fence onto the private land.*

**Kevin** Hey!

**Paula** Yeah?

**Kevin** You can't go on there.

**Paula** Why not?

**Kevin** Private property.

**Paula** Just exploring.

**Kevin** There's a bloke over there. Throw you off.

*Paula looks to where* **Kevin** *has pointed.*

**Paula** Can't see no-one. *(***Kevin** *comes through the fence.)* Is that a football?

**KEVIN** Yeah.

**PAULA** Give us a kick.

**KEVIN** Don't play with girls.

**PAULA** Who do you play with then?

**KEVIN** On me own.

**PAULA** One-man football?

**KEVIN** Used to have a lot of friends round here.

**PAULA** What happened?

**KEVIN** Got re-housed. Demolition. For the ring-road.

**PAULA** Give us a kick then?

**KEVIN** No.

**PAULA** Please yourself. *(She starts to go.)*

**KEVIN** Where you going?

**PAULA** Home to my brother.

**KEVIN** You got a brother?

**PAULA** Yeah.

**KEVIN** How old?

**PAULA** 'bout your age.

**KEVIN** Play football?

**PAULA** School team.

**KEVIN** What position?

**PAULA** Attack.

**KEVIN** *(really interested)* You live round here?

**PAULA** Just moved.

**KEVIN** I'm a goalie. D'you think he'll play with me?

**PAULA** If you want.

**KEVIN** Course I want! Will you tell him?

**PAULA** If you let me have a kick of your ball. (**Kevin** *kicks the ball over.* **Paula** *flicks it up onto her knee, flicks it from side to side a few times and passes it back to him. He gapes.*) He's a great swimmer too, my brother. Going in for a medal.

**KEVIN** Racing?

**PAULA** Life-saving.

**KEVIN** Wanna bit of chewing gum? (**Paula** *holds out her hand. He throws her a piece. She catches it.*) My name's Kevin.

**PAULA** My name's Paula.

**KEVIN** *(furtively excited)* Guess what I just seen?

**PAULA** What?

**KEVIN** Spastic.

**PAULA** Where?

**KEVIN** In a wheelchair. *(He starts grunting and shaking.)* Ugh, ugh, ugh … Oi'm a spastic. Ugh … Give us an ice-cream!

*(Same joke. He roars with laughter. She does not.)*

**PAULA** I don't think that's funny at all.

**KEVIN** You got to laugh though, haven't yer?

**PAULA** No.

**KEVIN** They don't understand anyway. They're mental!

**PAULA** What do you know about it?

**KEVIN** Don't get so ratty! Hey! Here he comes again!

*He turns away from* **Chris***, who has re-entered.* **Paula** *makes a quick* *motion with her hand to **Chris** to remain where he is.*

**Paula** How d'you know he's spastic?

**Kevin** Use your eyes!

**Paula** How d'you know he's mental?

**Kevin** They all are.

**Paula** Let's go and ask him.

**Kevin** Eh?

**Paula** Why not?

**Kevin** Well …

**Paula** Come on, why not?

**Kevin** I won't know what to say to him.

**Paula** He won't bite you.

**Kevin** I know he won't bite me!

**Paula** What's the problem then?

**Kevin** I ain't never spoken to one before.

**Paula** I thought you knew all about them! *(she calls to **Chris**)* Here!

**Chris** *(uncertain)* Yeah?

**Paula** *(She goes over.)* It's all right. This is Kevin. I've just met him. *(to **Kevin**)* Say hello then.

**Kevin** Mm … *(He gulps.)* … Hello then.

**Chris** Hello.

**Kevin** *(to **Paula**)* What's his name?

**Paula** Ask him.

**Kevin** What's your mm … what's your … what's your … what's your name?

**Chris** Have you got a stammer?

**Kevin** No. Why?

**Chris** I was just wondering why you were stammering.

**Kevin** *(to **Paula**)* Do you know him?

**Paula** His name's Chris.

**Chris** *(to Paula)* What about him?

**Kevin** Kevin. *(to **Paula**)* Why don't he speak to me?

**Paula** 'Cos you don't speak to him.

**Kevin** Whose side are you on?

**Paula** My brother's!

**Kevin** Is he your brother!

**Paula** Yeah, of course he is.

*Kevin stares at **Chris** for a moment, embarrassed and bewildered. Then the penny drops.*

**Kevin** Oooooooooh! You never told me you had two brothers!

**Paula** I haven't.

**Kevin** Eh? *(He beckons to her to tell her something in private. In a low voice.)* I want to ask you something.

**Paula** What about?

*Kevin nods in the direction of **Chris** and jabs with his thumb madly.*

**Kevin** Him.

**Paula** Well ask him then.

**Kevin** Can't.

**Paula** Why not?

**Kevin** *(mouthing; no voice)* Well! You know!

**Chris** Has he lost his voice or something?

**Kevin** No!

**Chris** I thought for a minute you'd gone dumb.

**Kevin** Nothing wrong with my voice, you really a spastic?

**Chris** No.

**Paula** What did I say?

*Kevin stares at Chris, thoroughly confused; then after a pause the penny drops again.*

**Kevin** Ooooooooh! I get it! You been having me on, you can't walk when you can! Nice one! Good trick! *(He goes to the fence.)* Here, come on in! *(Chris wheels through the fence.)* Fantastic! *(He thumps Chris playfully on the shoulder.)* What did you say your name was?

**Chris** Chris.

**Kevin** Kevin. Come on then! Out of your chair, I want a go!

**Chris** Look, I can't get out. I can only walk with crutches.

**Kevin** *(over Chris to Paula)* You mean he really is spastic?

**Paula/Chris** *(simply)* No.

**Chris** What I was born with is called spina bifida. My legs are lame.

*Kevin looks confused for a moment.*

**Kevin** Of course! What am I talking about? *(He taps his skull.)* You're not stupid, are you! Like, I mean, spastics …

*He goes into his spastic routine but Chris cuts him off very quickly.*

**Chris** And spastics aren't stupid either! They're as bright as I am, they've just got problems talking!

**PAULA** Right! The only people who are stupid are the stupid people like you, who make stupid jokes about spastics!

*Kevin stands there embarrassed for a moment.*

**KEVIN** *(over Chris to Paula)* I thought you said he could swim.

**CHRIS** *(to Paula)* Why don't he talk to me? Why does he always have to say everything to you?

**PAULA** Oh! Was he talking to me?

**CHRIS** He asked you a question.

**PAULA** He asked me a question?

**CHRIS** He asked you a question.

**PAULA** What question?

**CHRIS** I dunno. He didn't ask me the question.

**KEVIN** *(pointing)* I asked her the question! About you!

**CHRIS** *(pointing)* Oh! He asked you the question! About me!

**PAULA** Ooh! *(pointing)* He asked me the question! About you! *(to Kevin)* What was the question?

**KEVIN** Whether he could swim.

**CHRIS** Will you tell him, the answer to his question is yes.

**KEVIN** All right, I get it, sorry, apologise! Right?

**CHRIS** Will you tell him, his apology's accepted?

**KEVIN** *(jabbing his own chest)* Talk to me!

**CHRIS** I can swim a quarter of a mile.

**KEVIN** Without legs!

**CHRIS** Well, I do take 'em with me! I don't just cut 'em off and leave 'em on the bank!

**KEVIN** I can't even swim with legs!

**Chris** Aaaaaah!

**Kevin** What?

**Chris** What a terrible handicap!

*They all laugh.* **Paula** *takes the ball from* **Kevin** *and throws it to* **Chris**.

**Paula** Here you are, Chris.

*He heads it.*

**Kevin** Pretty good! Bet you can't get one past me, though. *(He lines up against the fence as goal and throws the ball to* **Chris**. **Chris** *heads it back.* **Kevin** *pretends to save it but lets it in.)* Great goal! Fantastic!

**Paula** Eh! You didn't even try to save it!

**Kevin** I did!

**Chris** You think I can't score past you.

**Kevin** You just did!

**Chris** I mean properly!

**Paula** If you kick the ball as stupidly as you play in goal, no wonder no-one'll play with you!

**Kevin** I can kick the ball hard!

**Chris** How hard?

**Kevin** This hard! *(He boots the ball as hard as he can. It flies away across the building site. He runs after it, then stops and turns.)* Oh no! There's that bloke coming back again! He's picked up the ball.

**Paula** Ask him for it then.

**Kevin** He said he'd call the Police!

**Chris** Against us?

**Kevin** Not you! He thinks you're simple. Here he comes!

**CHRIS** Hide! Hide!

*Paula and Kevin run off and hide. Chris stays where he is. Kevin pokes his head out of hiding.*

**KEVIN** Hurry up! He's coming!

*Paula runs to fetch Chris.*

**CHRIS** I know! Get in! Paula!

*She runs back and hides. Moody appears with the ball.*

**MOODY** All right, where are you, you little monkey? Come on! *(He sees Chris and speaks to him as if he's very simple.)* Have you … seen … a little boy? *(Chris nods.)* Where? *(Chris taps his chest.)* No! I mean … with a football!

**CHRIS** Oh! *(He points at Moody.)*

**MOODY** No! Me not a little boy! You … a little boy!

**CHRIS** Oh!

**MOODY** I'm looking for a naughty little boy.

**CHRIS** Eh?

**MOODY** Naughty! You know … *(Chris shakes his head. Kevin and Paula are now peeping out.)* Naughty! Like they go … *(He puts his tongue out.)* Or … *(He puts his thumb on his nose and waves. Chris looks bewildered.)* Or … *(He jumps up and down, screaming like a baby. He picks his nose and eats it.)*

**CHRIS** Eh?

**MOODY** Or … *(He shoves his bottom in the air and gives a loud farting noise.)* … which is very naughty and deserves a smack.

**CHRIS** Eh?

**MOODY** A big smack! *(He holds out his hand.)* Smack! *(Chris smacks it hard.)* Ouch! Not me! A little boy … *(Chris points to himself.)* …

With a football! *(Chris holds his hand out for the football.)* Yeah, that's right! *(He gives Chris the football.)* Have you seen one?

**CHRIS** Eh?

**MOODY** Seen one!

**CHRIS** Eh?

**MOODY** Have you … *(He points to Chris.)* … you …

**CHRIS** Yeah?

**MOODY** Seen a little boy with a football?

**CHRIS** Yeah!

**MOODY** Where?

**CHRIS** Here!

*Chris holds up the ball and points to himself.*

**MOODY** Noooooooooooo!

**CHRIS** Yeeeeaaaaaaah!

**MOODY** Oh forget it! Some people! Cor, I don't know! Dear me!

*He goes off muttering to himself furiously. **Kevin** and **Paula** come out of hiding. **Chris** waves to them to hide behind his wheelchair, then calls after **Moody**.*

**CHRIS** Hey you!

**MOODY** *(off)* Yeah?

**CHRIS** Anyone who acts like you needs his head looking at! Thanks for the football! Run!

*They run off, pushing **Chris**. **Moody** runs on.*

**KEVIN** *(puts his head round the corner)* Terrific, eh!

# *Staging the extract*

## SET DESIGN

The setting for this scene is a footpath that runs alongside some private land. The land, fenced off with "Keep out" and "Private Property" signs, is going to be turned into a car park but in its present state, it makes an ideal place to play football. There are two entrances in this setting, one from the footpath through a gap in the fence and one inside the area from a nearby security guard's hut. There also needs to be two different entrances onto the footpath.

◆4a **Solving the staging problems**

The following is a list of practical questions you need to answer in designing the setting for this extract. Go through the questions and find your own solutions to staging the scene. Experiment with scale drawings or models or in an actual performance space to find solutions to the staging problems.

1  Where is the audience in relation to the set? Where are you going to place the footpath and the hole in the fence? How big will the space be? Experiment with the shape and positioning of the path.

2  How will the fencing be supported to make it strong? What will it be made from? How are you going to make the hole look jagged but ensure that the actors will not hurt themselves on any jagged edges?

3  How will you make sure there is enough room for the wheelchair to get through entrances and exits and be turned in the space?

4  Where will Mr Moody enter and exit? Where will the two entrances/exits onto the footpath be?

CAMPAIGNS AND CONFLICTS

 ## PROPS

This is the props list for the extract:
- football
- sweets
- wheelchair
- chewing gum.

It is a simple list but you will still need to consider what kind of football, sweets and chewing gum you are going to use. The actors need to unwrap the sweets and chewing gum quickly on stage. You need to avoid sweets that will melt and make a mess. The actors need to speak and be heard while eating so the sweets should be fairly small and not too chewy.

The wheelchair requires careful research as there are many different types and the performer needs to be comfortable in it. If the actor playing Chris is a wheelchair user, he or she may well want to use their own. You will also need to find a football that is not too hard or likely to bounce all over the stage and into the audience. Letting some of the air out helps!

 ## COSTUMES

The parts of the 9/10-year-old children are intended to be played by adults. A young audience should be able to see themselves reflected in the characters on stage. You will need to find clothes that 9/10-year-olds wear now but in sizes that will fit actors of your own age.

◆4b **Costume research**

>
>
> [H] Tasks:
> - Find out from your own or a friend's younger brothers and sisters what they like to wear.
> - Look in home shopping catalogues to see what clothes are available for the age range.
>
> Chris and Paula's mother in the play does not have much money, so avoid 'designer' labels.
>
> Investigate the kind of uniform a security guard wears. You might be able to borrow one from a local security company.

**LIGHTING**

The scene takes place outside in broad daylight, so it needs plenty of bright light. You might be staging the play on tour in a school hall with no lighting at all, in which case make sure that all the curtains in the room are open.

 **SOUND**

A sound tape could be used to create an audio backdrop for the play. For example, the sound of traffic, passersby, road works, the wind in the trees, might help to establish that the scene is taking place outside.

# *Exploring the extract*

## HISTORICAL AND CULTURAL CONTEXT

This is what Roy Kift had to say about his play in 1981:

> 1981 has been designated as the United Nations Year of the Disabled (Ugh! Horrible word!) Person, and many theatres and groups around the world will be performing this play ... the play will probably be more effective in changing people's attitudes to the handicapped if it were performed in any year other than 1981. The problems facing us are enormous and much needs to be done to bring the handicapped out of the ghetto into a fulfilling life together with the rest of us. I can only hope that this play is a small contribution to this process, and look forward to the day when it has made itself redundant.

The play was written at a time when there was little or no recognition of equal opportunities for the physically or mentally disabled. More than 20 years on, the play is still far from redundant although things have changed to some extent. For example, all new public buildings must provide access for wheelchair users and many lifts position the operating buttons at wheelchair level.

### ◆4c Research and discussion

- Research into your school's policy regarding access for disabled pupils, teachers and visitors. How effective is this policy? Do the disabled feel integrated into the life of the school?
- Talk to any wheelchair user about how they manage to get around your school. How accessible do they find the building?
- Find out how non-wheelchair users behave towards the wheelchair users in your school. Ask both groups.

- Look up recent government legislation that aims to improve the quality of life for disabled people. How does the law protect the rights of the disabled?

In a recent radio discussion, a disabled actor was making the point that able-bodied actors were often cast to play the role of a character with a disability. The disabled actor went on to say that, while it is no longer acceptable to cast a white actor in the role of a black character, it is somehow still acceptable for an able-bodied person to play the part of a disabled person.

- How do you feel about this situation? Why do you think it happens? How are you going to go about casting the part of Chris in the play? How will you justify using someone without a disability in the role if it is cast in this way?

## GENRE AND SUBJECT MATTER

*Stronger than Superman* is written as a children's play. The purposes of the play are to educate and entertain a young audience about disability. *Stronger than Superman* deals with the issue by telling the story of Chris in a simple but open and honest way and increases understanding to overcome prejudice. In *Stronger than Superman*, Roy Kift informs his young audience about the disabled through the friendship that develops between Kevin, Chris and Paula. In one scene, for example, the audience finds out about how Chris has to use a colostomy bag to go to the toilet, but it is treated in a matter-of-fact way.

**PAULA** He had an operation, see. Because he was always wetting himself.

**KEVIN** Ugh!

**PAULA** And so to stop him doing it, he's got a bag. And all his ... water...

**CHRIS** Goes in there.

**PAULA** *(enthusiastically)* Hang on, I'll show you! *(She runs out. **Kevin** wheels up to **Chris**.)*

**KEVIN** And this bag... goes over your willy?

**CHRIS** No. They did an operation near my kidneys, here. *(He points to **Kevin**'s kidneys.)* Just under your belly button. And the water comes out through a hole into the bag. *(**Paula** comes back with the bag.)*

**PAULA** See! Just like a plastic balloon! *(She blows it up and waves it around.)* The water goes in this, and it all fills up. *(She sticks it in place on her belly.)*

**KEVIN** Ugh!

**PAULA** What's the matter with you then?

**KEVIN** My Mum and Dad say we don't talk about that sort of thing in our family.

**PAULA** Well, in our family we have to.

### ◆4d Finding out

> H
>
> Chris's disability in the play is spina bifida, but Moody calls him a spastic. Find out the difference between spina bifida and spasticity. What is offensive about the way the ice cream joke portrays spasticity?
>
> The word "spastic" is no longer used to describe people with this condition. What is the preferred term currently in use?

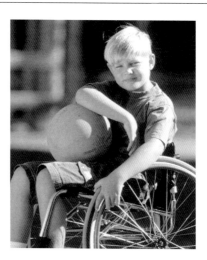

*This child leads an active life in a wheelchair*

**Stronger than Superman**

# *Exploring characters*

## KEVIN

Kevin's attitude to a wheelchair users changes from ignorance and fear to understanding and friendliness. This change begins to happen in the extract.

### ◆4e Still-image and thought-tracking

**in groups**

Look at the following sections in the script.

From **Kevin**: Guess what I just seen! To **Kevin**: Give us an ice cream! (Same joke.)

From **Chris**: Well, I do take 'em with me! To **Chris**: What a terrible handicap!

From (*Kevin and Paula come out of hiding*): To **Kevin**: Terrific, eh!

How has Kevin's attitude towards Chris changed throughout the scene?

Present each of these three moments as still-images or tableaux, demonstrating Kevin's change in attitude towards Chris.

Present the still-images again, but this time tracking the thoughts of each of the characters in the scene.

How does each of Paula's thoughts reflect her change of feeling towards Kevin?

What does Chris think about Kevin?

What are Kevin's thoughts about Chris in each of the still-images?

### ◆4f Hot-seating

Kevin starts off with one view about Chris, which is reinforced by Mr Moody. This slowly changes into a different view.

*cont...*

CAMPAIGNS AND CONFLICTS

> *Organization*: A volunteer takes the role of Kevin to answer questions put to him about his actions, motives and feelings. This person sits in the 'hot-seat' and must answer in role as Kevin. The purpose of the exercise is to try to understand the character's feelings and thoughts in the extract.
>
> *Evaluation*: Discuss the answers given by the person in the hot-seat.
>
> *Extension*: Repeat the exercise with someone in the role of Paula and then of Chris to find out about their feelings towards Kevin.

## PAULA

Paula is Chris's younger sister. Their relationship is just like any other between a brother and a sister but Paula is particularly supportive of Chris. Paula is also prepared to play a joke at Kevin's expense when she does not reveal to him that Chris is her brother.

### ♦4g Role-play

**In groups**

*Organization*: You need a wheeled office chair or a wheelchair if available. Working in pairs, one person is Paula and the other is Chris in a wheelchair. Others in the group are people out shopping. Create a space, which is cluttered with tables, chairs, other objects and people milling around.

*Situation*: Paula wants to get from one side of the room to the other, but has to get around objects and people in the way. Paula carries on a conversation with Chris, pushes him in the wheelchair, asks people to move out of the way and generally negotiates obstacles in their path.

*Evaluation*: How does it feel to be responsible for someone in a wheelchair?

## CHRIS

In this extract we see two sides of Chris's character. He behaves in one way towards Paula and Kevin but he acts differently with Mr Moody.

## ◆4h Cross-cutting

Cross-cutting can be used to show this difference in Chris's behaviour by playing two parts of the scene in parallel. The section with Chris, Paula and Kevin is labelled Part A and the section with Moody and Chris is labelled Part B.

*Organization:* Divide your performance space into two separate areas. Part A happens on one side of the stage and Part B happens on the other side of the stage. It is even more effective if you can use lighting so that you can cross-fade from one side of the stage to the other. Three actors are cast as Paula, Kevin and Chris in Part A. Four actors are cast as Paula, Kevin, Chris and Mr Moody in Part B. Part A and Part B are supposed to be happening at the same time on stage but the action and dialogue cuts back and forth between the two parts. Rehearse the cross-cut version of the extract that follows and perform it to an audience.

| Part A | Part B |
| --- | --- |
| PAULA Here you are, Chris. *(He heads it.)*<br>KEVIN Pretty good! Bet you can't get one past me, though. *(He lines up against the fence as goal and throws the ball to **Chris**. **Chris** heads it back. **Kevin** pretends to save it but lets it in.)* Great goal! Fantastic!<br>PAULA Eh! You didn't even try to save it! | |
| | MOODY All right, where are you, you little monkey? Come on! *(He sees **Chris** and speaks to him as if he's very simple.)* Have you… seen… a little boy? *(**Chris** nods.)* Where? *(**Chris** taps his chest.)* No! I mean… with a football!<br>CHRIS Oh! *(He points at **Moody**.)* |

88

89

| Part A | Part B |
|---|---|
| CHRIS  You think I can't score past you.<br>KEVIN  You just did!<br>CHRIS  I mean properly! | |
| | MOODY  I'm looking for a naughty little boy.<br>CHRIS  Eh?<br>MOODY  Naughty! You know ... (**Chris** shakes his head. **Kevin** and **Paula** are now peeping out.) Naughty! Like they go ... (He puts his tongue out.) Or... (He puts his thumb on his nose and waves. **Chris** looks bewildered.) Or... (He jumps up and down, screaming like a baby. He picks his nose and eats it.)<br>CHRIS  Eh? |
| PAULA  If you kick the ball as stupidly as you play goal, no wonder no-one'll play with you!<br>KEVIN  I can kick the ball hard!<br>CHRIS  How hard?<br>KEVIN  This hard! (He boots the ball as hard as he can. It flies away across the building site. He runs after it, then stops and turns.) | |
| | MOODY  Or... (He shoves his bottom in the air and gives a loud farting noise) ... which is very naughty and deserves a smack.<br>CHRIS  Eh? |

| Part A | Part B |
|---|---|
|  | MOODY A big smack! *(He holds out his hand.)* Smack! *(Chris smacks it hard.)* Ouch! Not me! A little boy... *(Chris points to himself.)* ... With a football! *(Chris holds his hand out for the football.)* Yeah, that's right! *(He gives Chris the football.)* |
| KEVIN Oh no! There's that bloke coming back again! He's picked up the ball.<br>PAULA Ask him for it then.<br>KEVIN He said he'd call the police! |  |
|  | MOODY Have you... *(He points to Chris.)*... you...<br>CHRIS Yeah?<br>MOODY Seen a little boy with a football?<br>CHRIS Yeah!<br>MOODY Where?<br>CHRIS Here! |
| KEVIN He thinks you're simple. Here he comes!<br>CHRIS Hide! Hide! *(Paula and Kevin run off and hide. Chris stays where he is. Kevin pokes his head out of hiding.)* |  |
|  | MOODY Oh forget it! Some people! Cor, I don't know! Dear me! *(He goes off muttering to himself furiously.)* |
| KEVIN Hurry up! He's coming! *(Paula runs to fetch Chris.)*<br>CHRIS I know! Get in! *(She runs back and hides.)* |  |

**CAMPAIGNS AND CONFLICTS**

| Part A | Part B |
|---|---|
|  | (*Kevin* and *Paula* come out of hiding. *Chris* waves to them to hide behind his wheelchair then calls after *Moody*.)<br>CHRIS  Hey you!<br>MOODY  (*Off*)  Yeah?<br>CHRIS  Anyone who acts like you needs his head looking at! Thanks for the football! |

What does this exercise tell you about Chris's character? Why does he behave the way he does towards Moody? How does the humour work in this scene?

### ◆4i  Improvisation – Over his head

Reread the following section of dialogue.

From **Kevin:** I thought you said he could swim. To Kevin: Talk to me.

This sequence illustrates the frustration that wheelchair users must feel when others talk to them through a third person. Wheelchair people often find that they are talked *about* rather than talked *to*.

*Organization*:  Person A is sitting in a wheelchair (or an ordinary chair), Person B stands to one side of the chair and Person C stands on the other side of the chair.

*Situation*:  Person A is in a café and is ordering some food and drink. Person B is A's friend. A is treating B to a meal in the café. Person C is the server. Throughout the improvisation, Person C must speak only to Person B and never to Person A.

**A (to C)**  What drinks do you have?

**C (to B)**  Does he/she want a menu?

**B (to C)**  I don't know. Why are you asking me…

*Evaluation*: How does it feel to be Person A or B? Why might Person C behave in this way? Was there any point in the improvisation when C felt inclined to talk to A directly?

*Extension*: Rerun the improvisation and work towards a point where C begins to talk directly to A.

Try the improvisation in different situations such as getting on a bus or buying clothes.

Change the role of person A to an authority figure, such as a bank manager or teacher. How does this alter the way C speaks to A?

## MR MOODY

Mr Moody is deliberately drawn as being ignorant and prejudiced against anyone in a wheelchair. The audience is not meant to feel any sympathy for him. The name the playwright gives him, Moody, describes his character. In the last scene of the play he is made out to be an even bigger fool, but the audience starts to see a glimpse of humanity in him when he agrees to let the children play on the land he is guarding.

### ♦4j Monologue

*Situation*: Imagine that Moody is in a pub telling his workmates what has happened to him in the extract. Write and perform a monologue that begins:

**MOODY**: There was this kid, see, and he was playing with his football up on the demolition site. I told him, I says, it's dangerous to play here…

## COMPARING TEXTS

**Richard III**
by William Shakespeare

**RICHARD OF GLOUCESTER**  But I, that am not shaped for sportive tricks,
Nor made to court an amorous looking-glass;
I, that am rudely stamped, and want love's majesty
To strut before a wanton ambling nymph;
I, that am curtailed of this fair proportion,
Cheated of feature by dissembling Nature,
Deformed, unfinished, sent before my time
Into this breathing world, scarce half made up,
And that so lamely and unfashionable
That dogs bark at me as I halt by them;
Why, I, in this weak piping time of peace,
Have no delight to pass away the time,
Unless to spy my shadow in the sun
And descant on mine own deformity:
And therefore, since I cannot prove a lover,
To entertain these fair well-spoken days,
I am determined to prove a villain
And hate the idle pleasures of these days.

This is Shakespeare's portrayal of a disabled character.

◆4k **Discussion**

> 1  How does this compare to the way a disabled person is portrayed in *Stronger than Superman*?
>
> Why do you think Roy Kift decided to make Chris's disability spina bifida?
>
> Why do able-bodied people often feel uncomfortable around severely disabled people?
>
> 2  The following extract is from a best selling crime novel that was also made into a film starring Denziel Washington. There have since been three sequels with Lincoln Rhyme, who is a quadrapedic, as the main character.

> Again Bank's eyes browsed Rhyme's body. Maybe he'd been expecting just skin and bones. But the atrophying had stopped not long after the accident and his first physical therapists had exhausted him with exercise...
>
> For someone whose muscular activities had been limited to his shoulders, head and left ring finger for three and a half years, Lincoln Rhyme wasn't in such bad shape.
>
> The young detective looked away from the complicated black ECU control sitting by Rhyme's finger, hardwired to another controller, sprouting conduit and cables, which ran to the computer and a wall panel.
>
> A quad's life is wires, a therapist had told Rhyme a long time ago. The rich ones at least. The lucky ones.
>
> Sellitto said, "There was a murder early this morning on the West Side."'
>
> (Jeffery Deaver 1997, The Bone Collector).

Compare this representation of a disabled person by Jeffery Deaver to the way Roy Kift represents Chris in the extract. How are they different? What does making a disabled person the main character in a best selling novel and the lead in a film tell you about society's attitudes today towards the disabled? Why are most people still uncomfortable in the presence of disability?

## ◆41 Writing and discussion

If you were writing a play in which an important character has a disability, which disability would you choose? How would you portray such a character fairly and interestingly? You might want to find out about theatre companies that include disabled performers.

CAMPAIGNS AND CONFLICTS

# *Exploring and comparing the four extracts*

## PROTEST

Protest is a way of getting a particular message across in trying to bring about social and political change.

- The women in *Lysistrata* mount a protest against the long war with Sparta.
- Emily Pankhurst speaks out for peace in *Oh What a Lovely War*.
- Both *The Crucible* and *Stronger than Superman* are forms of protests though less easily seen as such. Arthur Miller wrote his play as a kind of personal protest against Senator McCarthy's attack on freedom of thought and expression in 1950s America. Roy Kift's play exposes the prejudice towards disabled people and pleads for a change in social attitude.

◆5a **Improvisation**

*Organization*: Work in small groups to devise a protest play. You will need to decide what you stand for as a group. For instance:
- equal rights
- animal rights
- saving the environment
- a local issue.

*Situation*: You are going to meet with your local Councillor or Member of Parliament. You are going to produce fliers, posters and a list of points you wish to make.

*Opening line*: COUNCILLOR/MP: I can only give you five minutes of my time, but how may I help you?

*Evaluation*: How effective was your protest? Did you get your points across? Is he/she going to do anything for you?

*Extension*: Hot-seat the Councillor/MP for his/her response to your meeting.

# Exploring and comparing the four extracts

### ♦5b  Making an Exit

 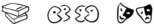

*Organization*: Work in small groups.

Identify the moments in each of the extracts when a character or characters leave the stage. Act out each of these moments from three or four lines before the exit up until the character(s) leaves.

In small groups, discuss the following points.

- How does the way the characters leave the scene differ between the extracts?
- What effect does a character who has left the scene have on those that remain on stage?
- What sort of atmosphere is created by the way in which a character exits from a scene? What different atmospheres are created by the exits across the four extracts?

### ♦5c  Witchcraft – discussion

1  To obey is better than sacrifice, and to hearken better than the fat of rams. For rebellion is as the sin of witchcraft.

(Samuel I; Chapter 15; verse 22.)

What does this Biblical quotation mean? How does it reflect the events in The Crucible?

2  **Lament for the Witches** by Caryl Churchill

> Where have the witches gone?
> Who are the witches now?
> Here we are.
>
> All the gentle witches' spells
> blast the doctors' sleeping pills.
> The witches hanging in the sky
> haunt the courts where lawyers lie.
> Here we are.

*cont…*

**CAMPAIGNS AND CONFLICTS**

> They were gentle witches
> with healing spells
> They were desperate witches
> with no way out but the other side of hell.
>
> A witch's crying in the night
> switches out your children's light.
> All your houses safe and warm
> are struck at by the witches' storm.
> Here we are.
>
> Where have the witches gone?
> Who are the witches now?
> Here we are.
>
> They were gentle witches
> with healing spells.
> They were desperate witches
> with no way out but the other side of hell.
> Here we are.
>
> Look in the mirror tonight.
> Would they have hanged you then?
> Ask how they're stopping you now.
> Where have the witches gone?
> Who are the witches now?
> Ask how they're stopping you now.
> Here we are.
>
> This song lyric from a play called *Vinegar Tom* asks the question, "Where have the witches gone?" How might you answer this question in respect of society today? Could the witch-hunts of Salem happen again? How are witches portrayed in this song? How similar or different is the impression given of witches in this song from that given in *The Crucible*?

### ◆5d Devised Performance

> The opportunity exists within your GCSE Drama Course to devise an original piece of drama. It is important when working on a devised piece to think about the structure of your work and to record any ideas that

you have as you go along. Remember that you need to communicate to an audience and you should consider the use of different aspects of drama that are appropriate (costume, set, lighting, sound, for example).

The following is a list of suggested starting points derived from the extracts in this collection.

- "Hell hath no fury like a woman scorned" *(The Crucible)*
- Using *The War Game/Pierrot Show* format of *Oh What a Lovely War*, devise a piece in a similar style using a different conflict (Vietnam, Falklands, Gulf War, World War II, Northern Ireland).
- Take the title of *Stronger than Superman* and devise a piece about a disabled Super Hero. Try to make the presentation like a cartoon.
- Devise a contemporary version of Lysistrata in which the wives and lovers of a terrorist group go on a sex strike until the men agree to give up their activities.

## THE PLACES

*Lysistrata* is set in Ancient Athens; *The Crucible* is set in 17th-century Salem in the USA; *Oh What a Lovely War* is set in London and on the battlefields of Europe and *Stronger than Superman* is set in the town or city where you live.

This is a page from a website illustrating a particular place.

**CAMPAIGNS AND CONFLICTS**

### ◆5e  Writing

**H**  Produce a similar web page for each location in the four extracts.

## WAR ZONES

*Lysistrata* and *Oh What a Lovely War* are both set during massive conflicts.

### ◆5f  TV or Radio News

*Organization*: Person A is a reporter from the battlefront between Athens and Sparta; Person B is a reporter from a battlefield of World War I. Person C is a newscaster in a TV or radio studio.

*Situation*: Person C announces the report from Person A and Person A gives their report. Person C then introduces Person B who gives a report.

*Extension*: Others in the group write news reports related to one of the extracts. For example, one reporter is at the Acropolis where the women of Athens are on a sex strike; another reporter interviews Sir Douglas Haig about his next military campaign.